'A close cousin   f the
most sweeping assessmen   oll.
Beginning with the sad fact of expendability in entry-level work, she
expands on Lauren Berlant's concept of cruel optimism, diving deep
into under-investigated histories to understand the roots of systemic
unhappiness and the nature of desire itself.' **Chris Kraus**

'A short, searing meditation on the idea of human replaceability in
politics and work, love and comradeship, which ranges from Karel Čapek
to Maggie Nelson, from Alexandra Kollontai to Lauren Berlant. It packs
an extraordinary range of ideas and inspirations into its brief polemic,
managing to be sensitive and yet utterly provocative.' **Juliet Jacques**

'How rare it is to read a book like Amber Husain's *Replace Me*, a work
of criticism that lays bare the horrors of our automated lives with such
subtle and sustained beauty. *Replace Me* is at once wonderfully unsparing
in its critique of capitalism's myths and wonderfully humane in its
affirmative vision of love's political vitality.' **Merve Emre**

'Essential reading for anyone in search of different futures.
Amber Husain's pellucid, erudite prose captures the many ways in
which the workplace has been changing, further eviscerating any sense
of engagement in meaningful labour. With verve and originality,
Replace Me tracks through time highlighting social discontents before
finally suggesting creative modes of coming to terms with, and hence
resisting, the chief dysfunctions of the present.' **Lynne Segal**

A catalogue record for this book is available from the British Library.

First published in 2021 by **Peninsula Press**

400 Kingsland Road

E8 4AA

London

peninsulapress.co.uk

Printed in Great Britain by CPI Group (UK) Ltd, Croydon

2 4 6 8 10 9 7 5 3 1

ISBN-13: 9781913512064

Replace Me
Amber Husain

-P

PENINSULA PRESS, LONDON
POCKET ESSAYS

For Izzie and Tom

'Some people cry out against the acceleration of time, others cry out against stagnation. They're both right.' **Henri Lefebvre**

My first experience of 'permanent' employment – a coveted job in publishing – was depressing for a number of reasons. I'd had jobs and been depressed before, but this job was special. It was the first on which I was able to rely for my subsistence, the first in which my contract wasn't built around the word 'casual', and the first which felt causally connected to my growing doubt about the beauty and meaningfulness of life.

The most obvious source of this malaise was the job's disappointing mundanity. The industry, its structure having calcified around a self-perceived fragility, had seemingly long since transformed editors into book production administrators, their interests in literature obsolete, imagination broadly shunned. Publishing decisions were based with hysterical circularity on what had been successfully published before, and the role of the editorial assistant in facilitating this was as absorbing as the season's master spreadsheet.

Assistants sent proposals to experts for obligatory but perfunctory review; recorded 'projects', once accepted, as spreadsheet data; tracked their progress by occasional email and, skipping the inefficient step of reading, translated the relevant features of manuscripts into incomprehensible codes that would render them readable by software. The software did something known neither to the assistant nor even to the editor, whose job was limited to 'acquiring' abstract book ideas and claiming these as figures on an annual list of things acquired. Editing itself, along with production, fell to outsourced workers in Chennai. I spent a full year in that publishing house and am not sure I ever saw a book.

More depressing still than mundanity itself was the way the job's deliberate mundanification stripped the assistant of any power. While garnished with the luxuries, then novel to me, of office perks, holiday pay and the chance to work entire days while seated, working as an editorial assistant returned me to the impotence I'd known, and had hoped one day to transcend, when working in restaurants and bars. No one was better at clarifying this than Nicole from HR.

Nicole was an embodied spirit of the 'Professional Managerial Class' – materially close to the workers but symbolically with the boss. Nicole was contractually mandated to respond with meaningful looks over the rims of her lemon-tinted glasses, which glared like the mean little headlights of some unaffordable car, to any assistant curious about the gap between their pay and the fabled London Living Wage. Her skill was to encourage through belligerent repetition our internalisation of the very forces we had supposed we might challenge upon entering her office – the forces that rendered us the company's most replaceable resources, and thus the most resourceless when it came to asserting demands.

Nicole would recite to us with eerie perspicuity the facts of our situation. The 'marginal value' we brought to the business had been steadily diminished by the number of available replacements. Our roles required minimal skills yet were subject to ferocious competition – did we not understand that, with the rise of automation, this was only likely to get worse?

Publishing, it seemed, was somehow standing on the threshold of a robot invasion. For all the evident pointlessness of what remained of our roles, we resolved that we ought to cling to them for fear of something possibly worse. For as long as we, the assistants, were replaceable, our condition of relative powerlessness could be continually upheld.

We quickly understood that the only raise on offer was that of Nicole's perfect brow. What followed was a kind of regressive enjoyment in the vapid but uncomplicated nature of our day-to-day working lives. Assistants, myself included, quickly warmed to the satisfactions of typing data into unfathomable bibliographic software, adding this unit of task-completion to tallies of tasks completed. We discovered new talents for doing this with messianic energy. Our knowledge that these tallies existed for no reason greater than themselves was stifled by the momentary pleasure of nevertheless having completed them. We began sincerely to describe new 'projects' as 'exciting'.

The reality of working while sitting on a chair was in some ways worse than the backache we'd experienced in previous jobs. Endurance asked for more than mere acceptance of myths; it asked that we join in constructing them.

*

The humanoid robot might commonly be thought of as an invention of twentieth-century science fiction, presaging a coming millennium of automated life, yet the so-called Beginning of Western Literature gives us just such a figure. In the eighteenth book of Homer's *Iliad*, a fleet of automated women are described at work in a forge in the sky. Built from lifeless gold but gifted the living energy of adolescents, these robots exemplify capacities (for fluent but restrained speech; fast but graceful movement) such as a mortal factory owner merely dreams.

Their master is the blacksmith god Hephaestus, a figure of advanced insecurity. Hephaestus has been out to prove himself since childhood when his mother threw him in the sea – an effort to conceal from heavenly society her son's 'defective' legs. Since he lacks the looks or athleticism of other Olympian gods, it is instead as a captain of industry that he makes himself indispensable – founder of a skyborne hub of production on which the others will rely. Hephaestus establishes a field in which to name himself unrivalled – god of fire, exemplar of skill, patron of all craftsmen. Meanwhile a band of workers must support this sweaty individual, each one charming and durable, each interchangeable with the next.

Power and replaceability have long been mutually constructed. Indeed, central to the *Iliad*'s premise is a Greek king's horror at his wife's rejection for another, Trojan, man. None in Troy will rest until the usurpation is avenged – a transgression of those unspoken boundaries that define what and who can be replaced. Throughout the tale, the trading and sacrifice of interchangeable daughters, girlfriends and wives reaffirms the irreplaceability of Greece's men. These men are to their mortal women as a god is to his robot slaves.

Yet while many English words and concepts find their source in classical Greek, *robot* is not among them. The word doesn't appear in English until 1920, in the translation of Karel Čapek's play *Rossumovi Univerzální Roboti (Rossum's Universal Robots* or *R. U. R.*). Derived from the Czech for 'forced labour', a notion loaded with a history of violence, *robot* contains a historically contingent critique of industrial relations.

By the 1920s and '30s, renditions of automatable labour's exploitation, from Fritz Lang's *Metropolis* to Chaplin's *Modern Times*, resonated as more than poetic fantasies of godly indulgence. Vast economic systems cried out for increasingly technological regimes, whose growth – a thrill for business owners – came at a cost to their employees. In *R. U. R.*, workers have been replaced by robots which are 2.5 times more efficient. Yet while human workers are largely absent from Čapek's stage, their plight is clearly mirrored in the robots' own abuse. Allowed no interests or enjoyment in life 'they are *less* than so much grass'. For as employers' fantasies of automation gathered weight in modern Europe, so did their fantasies of workers as resembling machines – highly efficient, barely demanding, easy to replace.

In Homer's epic register, the (gendered) norm of exchangeable underlings is mired in a vision of the world where the overlord Zeus, weighing the fates of all mortals against each other, ensures that things play out as they *always would have been*. The structure of epic literature is cyclical, symmetrical. It hooks the maintenance of systems of power to an aesthetics of divine order and inherent 'human nature'. The narrative rings that structure epic verse are embroidered with repetition as though to enforce the cosmic logic underlying systems of domination – justice in cycles of vengeance and geometries of fortune.

Two and half millennia after Homer, Čapek seized on a vision of power relations as destabilising sites of class struggle – slow but directional antagonisms, tending towards upheaval. While Homer's Zeus administers fortunes from cookie jars of evil and blessing, Čapek brings the jars down to earth and suggests that the unfortunate might seize them. A few decades earlier, Marx had projected that a 'class for itself' would eventually awaken to its common interests; Čapek gave his robot revolt a year – 2000.

I started my first job in publishing in the mid-2010s, more than a decade after Čapek's prophesied insurrection. Needless to say, it was characterised neither by post-liberation bliss nor the zealous vim of any liberation-in-progress. However cushy the scene of deindustrialised work, the threat of imminent replacement now dangled above that too. Underlings were tamed by the forms of deskilling that the Taylorist 'science of work' had innovated in the 1910s for Fordist factory workers. Fred W. Taylor's management break-through had been to recognise the power that workers retained through their knowledge of the production process. If workers under-stand what management does not and acquire specific skills, they find themselves able to take liberties and to bargain over the value of their labour. Breaking the process down into meaningless chunks, splitting execution from understanding – these were the logics that underpinned our ignorance of what we were doing, making us more manipulable and, of course, easier to replace.

The Fordist compromise, however, had been and gone, having managed to ward off revolution. Profit crises from before our lifetimes had seen labour go wherever it was cheapest. Expectations around pay, working hours and what counted as 'exciting' were lowered; calls to resist this dwindled to the odd half-hearted mutter. Never having experienced an alternative state of affairs, the millennial graduate workforce rolled with archaic rhythms of existence. The capitalist system of which we were a part seemed determined from on high – an order within which our highest hope was to pursue our own relative excellence.

The graduate workforce of the 2010s had internalised the capitalist realism described by Mark Fisher as an 'anti-mythical myth'. Tracing the roots of the present beneath the rubble of antiquity, the Italian writer and mythographer Roberto Calasso pinpoints a transformative moment within the ancient practice of sacrifice. While in the practice's earliest form, the sacrificial victim was deemed irreplaceable, it later became acceptable to use a stand-in victim. In the mythos of the Trojan war a sacrifice had to be made before the Greeks could first set sail: the king had to kill his daughter for the winds to go his way.

Yet in certain tellings Iphigenia is snatched from the altar, replaced at the crucial moment with a deer of equal worth.

Such acts of replacement conform to what Calasso describes as a reduction of sacrifice to 'pure exchange'. This, he argues, immeasurably expands the power of those who trade. Indeed, as long as the exchange is 'fair', the irreplaceable beings who profit from these transactions do so without judgement, or even recognition. The violence of these acts of substitution comes to be obscured by the syntax of exchange, portending the imagined neutrality of the godless invisible hand. 'In the end', writes Calasso, 'the world will be inhabited only by substitutes, hence by victims unaware that they are victims, because the irreplaceable priest who raises the knife over them has no name and no shape'.

In more charitable moments, I think of Nicole from HR as just such a victim of the workplace's irreplaceable priest. The priest, an arbiter of rules in which Nicole had little stake, had nevertheless persuaded her that she'd do well to enforce them. In archaic Greece, operations of power were given imaginative form in the almighty gods – Hephaestus in his forge line-manages his robots; Zeus atop his special cloud arranges his human dolls. In the present, the 'big Other' – the 'symbolic structure presupposed by any social field', to use the wording of Fisher, drawing on Žižek and Lacan – struggles to assume any meaningful shape that might be held to account.

Those who now attempt to direct dissent at a fallible capitalist entity find themselves unable to wrestle such a figure down. Sometimes it will seem to take the form of a boss, yet this boss will prove extremely unavailable. 'Dirk', the irreplaceable priest of my first job in publishing, was indeed often spoken of but never once seen. I imagined him as the Platonic Form of office operations, the curve-edged man on the toilet door, shapeless architect of workplace norms, an A4 piece of paper.

As in Kafka's bureaucratic labyrinth, where an infinite regression of substitutes is all that constitutes the system, the 'big Other can never be encountered in itself; instead we only ever confront its stand-ins'. In my office one such stand-in was Nicole; in Kitty Green's 2019 film *The Assistant*, it is the grey, faintly oily suit brought to life by Matthew Macfadyen.

The Assistant follows an entry-level worker named Jane around the washed-out corridors of a New York film studio's outer offices. Here, from the darkness of morning until late at night, Jane spends her day attempting to appease one or more imagined authorities. For one, there is an omnipresent public eye on the studio's operations – the gallery to whom PR departments were invented to play. For Jane this involves quietly sanitising the absent boss's office – powder is swept from the desk, needles cleared from the bin, earrings pulled out the carpet and cum stains cleaned off the couch. Another is the boss himself, who is absent from the screen yet understood as the action's prime mover. Never once making it into shot, his presence is nonetheless felt in cascades of email and telephone apologies.

The Assistant's central action is Jane's decision to report, to HR, the absent boss's sexual coercion of a beautiful young intern. Enter Macfadyen, the guy whose role is to dismiss such disruptions. He maintains, with grim pleasure, the office's homeostasis – its collectively constructed order of power and quotidian abuse. Macfadyen reminds Jane that her sought-after job is contingent on cooperation – that others who might replace her have gone to better schools.

Critics have read *The Assistant* as a film about Harvey Weinstein, yet that particular man seems to me beside the point. The film shows us the extent of employees' involvement in the construction of Weinstein-like spectres and the role of a prevailing bureaucracy in enabling this process. The quest to reach the ultimate authority who might resolve such an issue as Jane's will never end, because, as Fisher observes, 'the big Other cannot be encountered in itself: there are only officials, more or less hostile, engaged in acts of interpretation about the big Other's intentions'. For as long as the office is ruled by such acts of collective interpretation, its logics are as unassailable as an Other who doesn't exist – an irreplaceable priest with no name and no shape, or what lies beyond a doorway that is always crossable but never right now.

My second job in books was for an art publishing house. This was a pasture that seemed greener than the first, defined in opposition to the forms of online media produced by the so-called 'third industrial revolution'. Insisting upon its own distinction from the realm of the popular, this company wove financial struggle into its very mythos. As such, managers were able to pre-empt complaints concerning pay with allusions to *challenging times* – 'times', I imagine, that pre-dated the infamous events of 2008.

In this whitest of white-collar professions, to demand any reason more specific would certainly not have been polite. Any young employee who broke these unspoken rules of politesse would be met, from across a jungle of stacked limited-edition prints, proofs and luxury binding samples, by the faintest twitch of an elder's wiry eyebrow. A twitch would be enough to remind the whinging youth that they'd better *remember their luck*.

Historically, recessions have produced less cordial dynamics. In 1934 the Marxist magazine *New Masses* ran a piece celebrating strike action at the Macaulay Company – a rare but important instance of collective bargaining within book publishing. The piece identified exploitation among 'the most unstable and deluded class in our social system' (i.e., the middle one) as the product of an 'aura of gentility' – a fantasy of bourgeois dignity regardless of the terms of engagement. This fantasy was blamed for the publishing professional's commonplace acceptance of degrading conditions and 'miserable' pay. For the Macaulay workers, however, the impact of the Great Depression on salaries (cut), overtime (increased) and upward mobility (blocked) had finally proved intolerable enough to mobilise dissent.

The rarity of this seemingly exceptional event speaks to the depth of certain workers' delusions of status, but also shows that such delusions can in fact be punctured. In contrast to those 1930s workers, my colleagues and I found ourselves invested in accepting the abuse of our own potential replacement, viewing replaceability as a fact with a natural outcome. Convinced of our lot as a simple product of *challenging times*, perhaps we could have taken more seriously that myth's internal contradictions.

A writer who thought himself well-enough known might demand an assistant meet him on a Sunday afternoon, only to regale her with half-imagined premises for never-to-be-written books. Thus he attempted to distract this minion from the absence of his 'work-in-progress', gobbling the remains of her unpaid time. While assistants who discussed their salaries were formally reprimanded for this 'breach of contractual propriety', daring to invoke the contract in exchanges with charlatan authors was viewed as an unthinkable, undignified betrayal of the profession's Jurassic manners.

The editor who commissioned these half-imagined titles was typically a man with large hands and a mystically 'sterling' reputation. And while he would cultivate a comradely rapport with his young, typically female, assistant, the contrast between their working lives was literally night and day. She, attempting to mitigate her ingrown replaceability, might feel obliged to read manuscripts in the still-dark hours of the morning, as though her accumulated office presence would somehow increase her value. He meanwhile, creating a notable scarcity in terms of his appearance, found himself only more valued for his aimless daytime excursions. You'd struggle to believe that he who rarely wasted time at a desk –

unless, that is, to put his name to others' work –
found these to be particularly *challenging times*
for his profession.

*

If the relationship between economic depression and workplace inequality is in fact more
a question of power than of fate, where does this
leave the robots, which since Čapek's time have
served as a powerful emblem of an unstoppable
flight towards human obsolescence?

The recent flourishing of anxiety about
automation takes place in the context of a
very real under-demand for labour. This widespread underemployment comes with the
ongoing slowdown of economic growth across
the West that has threatened such industries
as publishing for over fifty years. As Aaron
Benanav has argued, the relentless pushing
down of prices and wages could just as much
be blamed on a stagnant economy's falling
demand for production as on any robot-

facilitated over-productivity. Robots serve as convenient scapegoats for the profit-driven political decisions that lead to the immiseration of workers.

Henri Lefebvre noted as long ago as 1987 that 'production [now] produces change in such a way as to superimpose the impression of speed onto that of monotony'. What is in fact a monotonously unequal distribution of technological un- and under-employment comes to be framed as a merely unfortunate symptom of acceleration. The widespread adoption of this line warrants closer scrutiny. Benanav references the erection of billboards in San Francisco which, in response to demands for a $15 minimum wage, threatened to replace fast-food workers with touchscreens if any law granting such a demand were passed. Meanwhile in Europe, fast-food workers could be seen to be operating in relative harmony alongside touchscreen technology, and often for better pay.

Both automation discourse and the kind of 'science of work' that informs the existence of HR are technologies of power that turn on the intentional enforcement of replaceability. Both position replacement as a form of 'innovation': one proposes that inefficient systems be replaced by more efficient ones; the other suggests that more efficient systems are coming to replace humans. And yet, as Helen DeWitt so dexterously unpicks in her 2011 novel *Lightning Rods*, the contemporary hyper-replaceability of things, processes and people is rarely evidence of such brilliant invention as capitalist language suggests; corporate creativity rhetoric retells a tale as old as (wo)mankind.

Lightning Rods follows the crawl of a failed Electrolux salesman's mind as his boringly violent sexual fantasies gradually inform his invention of a seemingly novel employment agency. Pondering his lack of professional achievement, Joe arrives at the unremarkable realisation that men could be much more efficient at work if their daytime desires for impersonal sex could be carried out discreetly in the office.

The means Joe develops for facilitating this is a workplace infrastructure whereby women's naked 'bottom halves' are made available to male employees through a hatch in the wall of a disabled toilet. With recourse to this mechanism, ambitious male employees are able to purge themselves of the kinds of distracting energies that stifle their productivity and expose their companies to harassment lawsuits. Meanwhile women's 'top halves' are protected from view, the risk of any problematic feelings diminished by enforcement of anonymity. Establishing himself as an agent for 'Lighting Rod' workers – women who sign on to engage in this arrangement – Joe achieves success across the United States as the model established through his agency becomes a workplace norm.

Crucial to the functioning of the Lightning Rods proposal is the provision that, across participating companies, the hiring of every temporary employee must be outsourced to Joe's agency. How to guarantee anonymity, Joe reasons, other than to obviate any distinction between Lightning Rods and other female temporary staff? Not only must feminine labour bear the costs of this plan, but so does the plan then work to further feminise labour. The female worker is expected to be reliably productive – devoid, in contrast to her male counterparts, of all inhibiting desires. Her role, furthermore, in the company, which necessitates replaceable labour, normalises precarity across the gender spectrum.

In her *Theory of the Gimmick*, Sianne Ngai suggests that the invention of the Lightning Rod, a paradoxically permanent temp, exemplifies the gimmick form. The gimmick, she suggests, is a labour-saving aesthetic device that achieves so little with so much. With its overblown flourishes, the gimmick ensnares our attentive energy but directs it nowhere new, productive or worthwhile. Its convoluted process turns out to arrive at a predictable, capitalist result.

Joe's elaborate justification for something so ridiculous sounding as 'in-house outsourcing' cannot help but prime the expectation of ingenuity. It reveals itself, however – punchline-like – to be nothing more than common business practice. As Ngai points out, there is nothing fictitious about the arrangement whereby workers are staffed through temp agencies discreetly embedded inside a company. (Non-)employees are trained specifically for use in a single business, such as Warwick University (via 'Unitemps') and the Bank of America (via 'B&A Temps'). More familiar still, Ngai observes, is the system's banal implication that 'at bottom, capitalism's ultimate labour-saving device is quite simply a woman'.

One is not born, but rather becomes, replaceable. Which is to say that the endlessly replaceable precarious worker arises from specific conditions. This figure, gendered and racially marked, emerges not from the womb but rather from capital's distortion of twentieth-century attempts at progress.

While the 1960s and '70s saw demands for liberation, the crisis of post-war capitalism had given birth to an ideology that twisted these desires to the interests of neoliberal market relations. Women were allowed into the white-collar workforce only for that work to be feminised in all the most exploitative ways. Women asked collectively for sexual freedom, only to be given disingenuous protection from individual sexual grievance. The Taylorist science that had disciplined worker efficiency ceded to a system in which workers would come to discipline themselves, experiencing survival as a matter of personal choice. Bouncing between platforms to patch together wages, TaskRabbits and Deliveroo riders are sold the idea that these companies are conveniently replaceable to the worker, rather than the other way round. The gimmick of 'flexible', 'local' and 'autonomous' service provision normalises subcontracting as a form of 'employment'. Self-motivation wards off revolution and ensures, as DeWitt suggests, that whoever's at the bottom gets fucked.

According to the UK's Employment Rights Act of 1996, 'no employment relationship exists if a worker can substitute another person to do the work'. This has been exploited – beneath a veneer of 'innovation' – by businesses in which inherently replaceable workers serve platforms rather than employers, and therefore forego the (already shrinking) rights afforded to full employees.

Within this context, the chance to be exploited as a full-time editorial assistant comes to resemble a prize whose winner must be solemnly grateful. The less fortunate, casual worker meanwhile misses out on sick pay, holiday pay, parental leave or protection from injustice at the hands of those by whom they aren't employed but for whom they nevertheless work. Laws seem designed to enshrine obligations (say, of employers to employees) in a nationwide behavioural code. Yet while laws have been written to make norms of employment protect against excessive replaceability, it is instead replaceability that has come to govern norms of employment.

*

The well-known paradox of Theseus's Ship invites us to consider the extent to which stable forms not only withstand but rely upon replacement of their constituent parts. As each of its worn-out timbers is replaced over the years, does the boat continue to be 'Theseus's Ship', even by such time as none of the ship's original parts remain?

In retrospect, I look upon my moment with Nicole from HR as one of practical education, hinting at some of the systems at play beneath the casting of assistants as timbers. Much as we enjoyed our office perks and the limited rewards of tick-lists, the flimsiness of these luxuries served as evidence of wider rot. Brushes with Nicole were brushes with the truths beneath her evasions – moments of cognitive rupture in a year-long intellectual lunchbreak. At times such moments felt like calls to make a basic decision: side with labour as conditions declined for all but the profit-extractors, or make the best of our privileges and skip into the glades of the Nicoles.

While typically framed in philosophical terms as a problem of metaphysics, the question posed by Theseus's paradox is more, it would seem, one of politics. In the end its answer depends upon a judgment as to whom or what we think of as replaceable. To the Greeks the only irreplaceable priest in the frame was Theseus himself, or more accurately the valour his name symbolically conferred. But as Čapek tried to imagine in 1920, or as the staff of the Macaulay Company hoped in 1934, it is not beyond the realm of possibility for the ship to be reimagined – as no more sacred, irreplaceable indeed, than the unnamed workers who maintain it.

It is 2014 and, walking home from the club one morning, a friend who has now reached a point of near derangement with job-hunting sees that someone we bumped into on the dancefloor has just added him on LinkedIn.

Playing dip-and-sniff with what remains of a bag of K, my friend, his voice slowing and wobbling with the wind, starts to talk about how he's thinking of going into the sleep industry. 'I think sleep might be my thing', he says, which I put down to the fact that he is walking while significantly tranquilised.

The next day, however, I watch him demonstrate his sleep tracker – a dad-style accessory that has been allowing him to set 'sleep goals' before having his progress visualised for him in a variety of charts. This has given him the greatest sense of achievement he has felt in the six months since graduating.

Consensus among our ilk was that higher education had become a sort of computational device through which aggregates of school grades were fed to be processed and released as accumulations of yet further, more abstract, grades. The observation, by this point, appeared so mundane as to foreclose any thought of its resistance. Indeed, in light of what we found in their aftermath, we were relieved to have amassed these credits. We imagined the metrics of achievement assigned to each of our graduate peers would naturally convert into inputs in the function of job market worth. Those with less impressive statistics to their names sought to recuperate life points through alternative forms of numerical self-improvement.

The years in which my sleepy friend and I passed through that machine were particularly marked by the unlucky sign of the Quantified Self. Champions of this movement had cameras, recorders and nano-sensors installed beneath their skin. More prosaically, our watches and phones now monitored our reading speed, walking speed, sexual performance, pulse, intelligence, wit. Nor were the sources of data limited to those we produced while awake. Apps could apparently evaluate the success of our unconscious hours, movements and sounds betraying the duration and quality of our sleep.

To those confronted by the experience of replaceability so strategically enforced among entry-level workers, the Quantified Self represented a kind of counter strategy, turning replaceability into the solution. By exposing ourselves to what many believed to be the raw data of our existence, graduates of the 2010s were sold a sense of our own control of the common metrics that rendered us comparable with others. To master one's Quantified Self in this way was to bring oneself closer to the rarefied status of irreplaceable priest, optimised subject of an order that rewards the few who can outcompete.

The priests who led the way in this were making a lot of money. Some were doing so for reasons of putative virtue, under the banner of 'Effective Altruism'. 80,000 Hours, a charity set up in 2011 by a young Oxford philosopher, was initiated to help graduates choose careers in such a way as to maximise their power as philanthropists. It was founded on the heels of Giving What We Can, a charity dreamt up by the same founder two years earlier that used an algorithm to calculate the most efficient charitable use of 10 per cent of a giver's annual income. Central to this calculation was the 'argument from replaceability'.

The idea was that in assessing the positive impact of your career, an important consideration was the likelihood that 'if you hadn't taken the job, someone else would … have taken it instead'. This premise was derived from a vision of people, things and abstract phenomena – from human suffering to social good – as quantifiable and therefore numerically interchangeable. While the charity's representatives later admitted that 'it's very hard to know what would have happened if you hadn't taken the job, and therefore to quantify the importance of replaceability', they stood by the proposition that replaceability presented a case for 'earning to give'. The more you make, the more you can give; what's good for the individual, happily, turns out to be what's good for society.

In the early days of 80,000 Hours, this somewhat limited vision of change involved a careers service suggesting to subscribers that banking might be their optimally altruistic destination. The implication was that bankers could not only justify their accumulation of wealth as a prerequisite for generous giving, but could even thus claim it as an act of moral duty. Among those whose lives had been disfigured by the symptoms of poverty, 80,000 Hours identified the people whose suffering could most efficiently be mitigated with cash. Never mind that the actors supposedly best placed to meet this demand were, by virtue of the company's careers advice service, themselves architects of wealth inequality.

In so 'effectively' persuading its followers to reproduce a world damaged by the continual replacement of its damagers, such ventures attest to the power of quantification to impose an optics of progress on projects that systematise stasis. By 2015 the altruists Peter Thiel and Elon Musk had moved on from exploring wealth accumulation's potential for mitigating wealth inequality. Now their priority was investing in tech to solve the problem of a tech-born apocalypse. The circularity in such a move was outweighed, they seemed to think, by statistics. Understanding the value of preventing a total end to human life as relative to the number of lives it would save in a vast imagined future, no amount of suffering taking place now could justify similar investment. As Amia Srinivasan wrote in a fair-minded essay on Effective Altruism's philosophical poverty, 'Who doesn't want to believe that their work is of overwhelming humanitarian significance?'

Mathematical principles have been invested with beliefs relating to accuracy, precision and moral goodness since long before the neo-liberal era. The leftist activist and Christian philosopher Simone Weil particularly admired the ancient Greeks in their primordial reverence for numbers. For Weil, the gift of mathematics, limited in the twentieth-century West to deployment in questions of 'matter', had among the Greeks offered 'an apprenticeship to virtue'. For Weil the *Iliad*, depicting a 'continual game of seesaw', seemed to be a quintessential expression of moral balance, exemplifying a holy and unparalleled form of 'geometrical rigour'. Geometry, 'excluding all that is arbitrary or dependent on chance', came closer than anything else to the order of 'spiritual matters'.

By her own account, Weil was less interested in quantifying the self than in the self's renunciation. She made explicit the separation of numbers themselves from their use as units of capitalist value. She saw, however, the direction in which a fetish for numbers might lead. In *Gravity and Grace*, first published in 1947, she laments that the 'spirit, overcome by the weight of quantity, no longer has any criterion other than efficiency'. Imagine her despair had she lived to witness selves valued in accordance with earning power combined with weekly step count.

By 1988, with the publication of *The Mezzanine*, Nicholson Baker showed that this contemporary self was already beyond Weil's help, already the subject of such farce as supposedly follows the tragic. Howie, Baker's protagonist, embodies the confused neoliberal subject – a *homo economicus* whose instrumental reason will help him, he believes, to maximise the satisfaction of desires as though he too were a market. In the course of narrating a mere hour's worth of action (most of it the daydreaming registered on a single escalator journey), Howie offers a textbook's worth of unnecessary number crunching.

Having intended to read a copy of Marcus Aurelius's *Meditations* during his lunchbreak, Howie finds himself thinking less about the intricacies of Stoicism than about how many times each year he wonders whether Penguin are able to make money selling paperbacks. Referring to a table of thought-frequencies he has invented over lunch, he satisfies himself with an estimate of four. 'Merely saying that you often wondered something', he reasons, gives 'no indication of how prominent a part of life that state of mind really was'. Instead, he concludes, anybody wanting to understand the measure of themselves ought to quantify and rank the occurrence of each of their thoughts per year.

The impact of this kind of thinking on Howie's personal flourishing is captured by his torpor in the face of life decisions. Rather than engaging with these qualitatively, he fixates, as he does with all of his thoughts, on their rate of incidence per annum: 'Job, should I quit?' (34.0); 'Marriage, a possibility?' (32.0); 'DJ, would I be happy as one? (9.0). As such, Howie sees that while he is now technically a man, he is 'not nearly the magnitude of man [he] had hoped [he] might be'.

Demonstrating Howie's inability to distinguish which forms of quantification are worth his while manipulating, Baker has him soliloquise over several pages on the subject of replacing his broken shoelaces. As he attempts to calculate the precise balance in the shoelace-snapping event of such dynamics as 'chronic-walk-flex' and 'acute-pull-fray', Howie ironically rules out the notion that identical wear on both laces might be the symptom of a shoe tying routine 'so unvarying and robotic' as his own.

On the twenty-first-century market, Howie's style of transition from man to machine finds bounteous tools of expression. By the 2010s the bourgeois consumer could enjoy a variety of means of replacing not just their shoelaces, but the faculties with which they tied them.

While tech brand directors, shareholders and a handful of venture capitalists enjoy gigantic profits, we ask of their products very little in return beyond novel illusions of convenience. Why use a finger, we ask ourselves, to turn on the lights when an AI speaker could carry out this function with equal flair? Why gauge by eye the amount of coffee left in its container when a special container can sense the weight and order a replacement itself? Solutions appear to have been organised in advance of our registering problems. Somehow we have found relief in this as opposed to cause for mistrust.

Just before starting my first publishing job, I remember reading a now infamous study from Oxford University on 'The Future of Employment'. Ranking jobs from 1–702 as more or less susceptible to computerisation – 1 being the safest and editors seeming relatively unthreatened at 140 – it estimated that 47 per cent of all jobs were at 'high risk' of automation within two decades. This figure was based on data indicating the prevalence of technologies involved in the various industries under study. It has now been made clear that the researchers failed to distinguish between technologies used to *augment* human labour and those that, more threateningly, *substitute* for human hands. A more recent OECD study sensitive to this distinction recalculated the 'high-risk' jobs as a somewhat less sensational 14 per cent.

Homo economicus – naturally an ambitious, productive creature, finds himself nonetheless helpless in the face of his light switch and fridge. Perhaps he believes that his gimmicks, which hinge on the saving of reproductive labour, will genuinely serve to augment his productive capacity. Perhaps he believes this will deliver him from being surpassed by a robot. Replacement is the problem; replacement is the cure. The feminine-by-default voices of Alexa and Cortana and that nameless Google Home bride substitute for modern man's chore-doing faculties; or perhaps, more simply, for a wife. Subbing in for 'capitalism's ultimate labour-saving device', tech seems to serve us with novel ways of carving out bonus seconds, each to be dedicated diligently to labour market competition.

Those society lauds as visionaries tend to produce the most banal ideas. Confronting this paradox, the broadcaster Lizzie O'Shea writes that such people, 'who are satisfied with the basics of the present, who might quibble with the pace of change rather than its direction, often come up against the limits of their imagination'. As O'Shea implies, the best ideas for changing any system are unlikely to come from its beneficiaries.

Among the interventions within our culture of superficial change – among the rental rebellions and new frontiers in footwear – the 'meal replacement revolution' exemplifies these visionaries' blend of promise and deflation.

The guarantee that ignited the success of such meal replacement products as Soylent, Huel, Plenny and Purition – synthesised drinks each substituting nutritionally for one 'complete' meal – was that every hit of smooth beige pulp would translate into a measure of life-transforming efficiency.

According to the marketing copy, Huel delivers survival straight to your door. By 'taking a few things off our plates' and replacing them with 'a complete blend of everything the body needs', Soylent products turn the inconvenience of a meal into a 'one-step process'. The time saved on thinking about, cooking and eating food can be spent on more productive pursuits; drinkers can recoup whatever energy they have lost to a lifetime of suboptimal nutrition. This, the brands tell us as they ooze through society, is the definitive 'future of food'.

Such rhetoric is not without precedent. In 1930 Filippo Marinetti, the founder of Futurism and early adopter of Italian Fascism, advanced a new model of eating through his *Manifesto of Futurist Cooking*. This model formed part of a larger project of rejecting the values and mores that, in Marinetti's opinion, had condemned pre-Mussolini Italy to 'lassitude, pessimism, nostalgic inactivity and neutralism'. Focusing on the nation's potential, in an era of industrialisation, to cultivate methods of streamlining in life as in work, Marinetti's infamous pasta ban was but one minor step in a movement that envisaged 'plastic complexes' as replacements for 'natural' food.

Just as the Futurists spread their politics through the bourgeoisie by means of reification in the fine art object, Soylent led in the crafting of an aesthetic to match its 'futuristic' agenda. Its clean visual identity – block pastel colours and sideways sans serif fonts – was devised by an artist-founded design and marketing firm to suggest such familiar virtues as purity and precision. The copy on a can of Soylent is uniformly clear of clutter, limited to little more than scaffolds of neat nutritional figures. Stacked in clean lines, they smugly repeat the proportion of the drinker's ideal daily requirement (20 per cent, 20 per cent, 20 per cent, 20 per cent) supposedly fulfilled by each ingredient. Just as minimalism sought to supersede expressionism's complex scrawls, the meal replacement appeals to the ideal of concept without the baggage of excess substance, a practice of eating with the mind.

Such aspirations are summarised in the work of artist (and former Soylent employee) Sean

Raspet, who has sought to position the meal replacement product as an exhibition *objet*. In a 2015 collaboration with the Swiss Institute and Pantone, Raspet presented a signed, editioned run of Soylent's 'Technical Food' and 'Technical Milk' flavours as part of an exhibition reviving Corbusier's 1925 model home installation *Pavillon de l'Espirit Nouveau*. In the Swiss Institute's twenty-first-century update of that home, its furnishings fresh from the 3D printer, the need for anything so suggestive of bodily function as a kitchen was concisely overturned by twin Soylent dispensers positioned astride the front door. It was, it seemed, a return to the call for a brutalist 'dwelling machine', which (with reference to Buckminster Fuller's 1927 *Dymaxion House*) the chairman of the American Architectural League described in 1929 as a machine 'with replacement value, a machine which can be set down practically in any location'.

In 1935 Walter Benjamin attributed the public's ready acceptance of art as endlessly reproducible to a growing 'sense of the universal equality of things'. By equality we can here read 'commensurability', a logic that allows one thing (say, food) to be numerically evaluated (as nutrition) and hence replaced (by an equivalent source of nutritional value). 'Thus', he writes, 'is manifested in the field of perception what in the theoretical sphere is noticeable in the increasing importance of statistics'.

Now, as in 1935, the notion of any statistical 'truth' of nutrition remains implausible (the 'perfect' diet being subject to perspective and endlessly incomplete knowledge). A consumer, however, will trust in the accuracy and seeming transparency of a grid of numerical information, even as the colourless, odourless liquid in the can reveals nothing to support its veracity. A list of unfamiliar ingredients – biotin, gellan gum, isomaltulose – and assurances of a daily measure of selenium, molybdenum and pantothenic acid succeed in signifying Soylent's nutritional excellence without having ever meant anything to the Soylent consumer before. Similarly Huel's ingredients list boasts a 'micronutrient blend' with its own list of opaque constituents longer than the master list in which the blend itself appears.

Indeed, the consumer will make infinite illogical leaps to justify outsourcing their feeding to a tech brand. In 2019, a think-piece in the *New Statesman* celebrated meal replacements for enabling 'feminists' to 'take back time lost to pressures and constructs of the patriarchy'. Examples of these pressures and constructs included 'putting on makeup' and 'worrying about planning outfits'. If Taylorism depended on the measurement of productive time to discipline workers, women a century later were measuring consumptive time to effectively discipline themselves.

Rather than challenging social expectations she considers patriarchal, the Huel feminist ensures she is ready to thrive among them; she only has to give up food. Can it be that a society where 'time is money' has blinded people to any dimension of a task beyond the time and money taken to complete it? Have we all become Howies whose tabulations of thought-frequency threaten to eclipse actual thought?

If my anorexic teens are anything to go by, the success of the meal replacement hype is more than a simple case of its appeal to economic logics. Its achievement has been to reabsorb a specific, dissenting desire into this conservative project. 'For too long', the founder of Huel declares, 'we have made food so delicious that we crave it', which seems, at first, like a mysterious way to sell an edible product. Yet histories of self-starvation have shown with remarkable continuity how renunciation itself can gather a hot, propulsive appeal.

It's commonly believed that the anorexic subject has lost all desire for food. This take is linguistically supported, with *an-orexis* denoting, in Greek, a basic absence of appetite. In *The Neutral*, Roland Barthes muses that if there is a specifically anorexic desire, it is perhaps a kind of 'inappetite' – a want for precisely nothing. It is a want, he supposes, that comes from society's imposition of bounty – its leaving of nothing to be desired but a strange desire for the void. I doubt he can have spent much time with anorexics, many of whose typical psychic day consists in the meeting of a holy hunger with elaborate, juice-drenched dreams of its undignified fulfilment; whose desire for nothing co-exists with a capacious appetite for food. Still, it seems there is truth in this idea of 'nothing' as a positive object of want.

Simone Weil, more intimately acquainted with the self-starver's quirks, suggested that hunger could itself be the seed for kind of renunciative ecstasy. 'We have to fasten onto the hunger', she declared like a ravenous mutineer – there 'must be no compensation'. For Weil, attention to this 'void' without intention of its filling was a means of fulfilling desire for the (outward-looking) 'good'. In trying to fill the void, she thought, we fall prey too quickly to our minds. The void, by contrast, is a place entirely empty of self-projections, attachments to personal prestige and other such consolations. To her mind, this desire for suspension in the void was a kind of transcendence of ego – a means of escaping the sensibility that shackled man to his 'self'.

In *Aliens and Anorexia* (2000) Chris Kraus alights on Weil's starvation journey to suggest that anorexia, rather than being the sickness of a 'simpering solipsistic dog', might instead be a valid form of resistance to the dominant ideology. She posits that Weil, equating food with 'the *entire social order*', enacted through starvation a political rejection with equally expansive scope.

And yet, in view of the trajectory that brought Weil to her early death, I wonder if self-starvation of this seemingly limitless kind can ever be entirely redeemed of its egocentric structure. While self-annihilation might be a weapon of those whom this order has designated 'lower', and one with an aesthetics of defiant ego-transcendence, it nevertheless remains a project of finding solutions in the self, one in which the normative will to be outstanding infiltrates even the struggle against such normative injunctions.

Weil was dead by the age of thirty-four, having limited herself to the precise number of calories available to her countrymen in occupied France. Though a lifelong activist immersed in collective struggle, in her death she was, it seems to me, closer to a lone martyr – not a typical religious practitioner of controlled collective fasts, but rather an exemplary artist of starvation's logical telos. Step counts may have been absent from her figurations of self-worth, yet calories came to guide her to a curiously pointless death.

Much of my sixteenth year was spent, rapt by the guidance of digits, counting out raisins in sixes. While doctors measured my BMI, ovaries and heart rate (slowed to the mere suggestion of a beating instrument), I myself regulated gulps and grams, kilometres covered on foot, and minutes spent in stillness. If the loss of hair and friends that accompanies the shedding of too much weight constitutes any source of sadness, its downsides, I felt, were convincingly outweighed by distance from a certain kind of body. Numerical distance, I mean to say, from a body within mortal 'range', which in its ordinary fleshiness betrays its own miserable needs.

Anorexics who undergo treatment are offered replacement meals to restore their wasted bodies. Ensure and Fortisip are the clinical brands of choice in this project of temporary compromise – palliative calorific slop pre-scribed to the elderly and sick. Designed with no greater thought for aesthetics than a packet of ibuprofen, these supplements bypass the shame of food in all its attachment to desire. The patient who consents to this regime of re-feeding needn't submit the disease itself to any kind of radical challenge. They have found a replacement for the object of shame that imprisons the replaceable masses, food representing the weakness of mortals who can't be irreplaceable priests. We might interpret Huel as a co-optation of anorexic dissent, but there is also an inherent likeness as old as individualism itself. In both renunciative woman and the Silicon Valley bro we find, if not necessarily a simpering solipsism, a compliance with the rules of a game that whispers of salvation in personal exception.

In his 1903 account of industrialisation, techno-optimist George S. Morison wrote of engineers as 'priests of material development'. The tech engineers behind Silicon Valley's meal replacement brands continue to elevate themselves to such heights of irreplaceable priesthood. When Soylent's founder first took to his blog to extol the benefits of 'giving up food', he wrote of how transcending his lowly desire to eat had lent him superhuman talents for reading, thinking and 'noticing' art. It had also cured his dandruff.

But as Weber once pointed out, priests are not the same as prophets. While prophets disavow old narratives and propose new ones, priests oversee what already prevails, maintaining age-old norms. Tech's replacements and prostheses have promised to 'augment' human potential, yet what is really augmented by efficiency-centric products? Sold as one-size-fits-all tools for cultivating exception, products such as these enhance little more than familiar values and delusions. The fact that there are Futurist echoes in contemporary meal replacement brands re-emphasises this point. It signals a definite 'pastness' that, through products like Soylent, continues to condition the present.

Early in *Rossum's Universal Robots*, Helena – a unionist figure from the 'League of Humanity' – suggests to the factory owner that the robots might receive a wage, giving them access to whatever it is that robots might want. 'What would be the point of that?' the incredulous managers ask; robots, for obvious reasons, have not been designed to desire. 'You can feed them on pineapples, straw', they cry, 'It's all the same to them'. While the robots are programmed to experience pain (a reflex for avoiding damage), pleasure has no place in the agenda of endless (re)production.

'It is human misery and not pleasure which contains the secret of divine wisdom', wrote Weil. To her mind, the exhausting experience of labour – 'to work in order to eat, to eat in order to work' – was something we should simply accept and endure, finding solace and distraction in beauty. It seems as though her acceptance of the hardship involved in struggle found itself feeding the interests of a distinctly ruling class. An interest in ensuring the oppressed assume responsibility for themselves. Rather than turning desire towards the transformation or abolition of work we are invited to turn within ourselves to seek some means of its 'transcendence'. 'Workers', Weil declared, 'need poetry more than bread. They need that their life should be a poem'.

The winning of freedom demands that we are able to detect our own desire for oppression. Suppose the workers of today were offered, instead of misery and poems, their freedom from the fears and fantasies of replacement that animate their lives, resigning them to worsening labour conditions while breeding dreams of individual excellence. As Weil herself once declared, a useful critique of a civilisation should seek to unravel the imprisonments we habitually disguise as freedoms. It should try, she wrote, to expose 'the trap which has made man the slave of his own inventions'. Decrying the Futurist, Fascist resolve to make an art of violence, Benjamin took this as 'proof that society has not been mature enough to incorporate technology as its organ'. Like Weil he saw worrying evidence of a humanity able to take pleasure in the spectacle of its own destruction.

In 2019, *Frieze* magazine commissioned its own 'Futurist Cookbook' with the aim of reinspiring the kind of 'optimism' it attributed to Marinetti's project of the 1930s. Despite this somewhat questionable premise, a contribution from the artist Otobong Nkanga offered a refreshing response. Painting a molecular structure in acrylic on paper, Nkanga described the assemblage as a *Recipe for Repairs*. Defining 'repair' in her accompanying text, she summarised her take on 'optimism' in a set of lexical possibilities:

> 1a: restore by replacing a part or putting together what is torn or broken
> b: restore to a sound or healthy state
> 2: make good/compensate for/remedy

Nkanga interprets the replacement object as an item of restoration rather than progress. Like Ensure – a humble, medicinal surrogate meal for the old and infirm. Casting aside the posture of Ensure's techno-utopian spin-offs, the work invites the optimist to consider the limits of Futurist ideology. Marinetti may have seen his proposed regime as a matter of historic rupture, but, for the dangerously underweight child, Ensure never sought to be the Future of Food.

While the Futurists were pushing 'plastic complexes' as human-augmenting replacements, a French-Russian surgeon named Serge Voronoff was making vast sums of money in 'rejuvenation by grafting'.

'Grafts', as practiced by Voronoff, were surgical replacements of middle-aged reproductive organs, first with testicles taken from prisoners (killed before their balls had a chance to age) and later from chimpanzees. In ladies Voronoff implanted the ovaries of juvenile monkeys – a procedure reportedly in high demand.

The Russian writer Mikhail Bulgakov fictionalises Voronoff's patients as the affluent subjects of his 1925 novel *The Heart of a Dog*. Bulgakov's surgeon is a man named Philip Philipovich, who like Voronoff is known for his lucrative trade in animal-in-human transplantation. Here he has built a playground for fantasies of self-reconstruction.

In one of the novel's early scenes the titular dog, himself condemned to implantation with a Bolshevik's testicles and pituitary gland, looks on as Philipovich inspects his regular visitors. An older man, his wrinkles corrugating 'skin as pink as a boy's', is discovered to have perfumed his underpants in the hope of impressing young girls. A woman whose neck, crumpled and slack, betrays her advanced years shrieks in desperation for the love of a younger man.

'I swear, if you knew the agony I've been through', she cries, lamenting how his gaze has been ranging elsewhere. The crumple-necked woman, we understand, is afraid of being replaced.

In any society that fetishises youth, the basic experience of ageing (supposedly common to all) becomes the individualised experience of creeping and unholy obsolescence. Written during the NEP period that followed the Russian Revolution, *The Heart of a Dog* depicts in its wealthy cast a type concerned with the opportunity to take back control – to claw back some of the personal advantages threatened by the Soviet regime of redistribution.

In the contemporary capitalist West, the industry in youth pervades all corners of society. Indeed, while rejuvenation by grafting may no longer be a thing, among today's wealthy Californians there exists a market for transfusions of teenage blood. Marketed youth, as Mark Greif put it in his 2006 essay 'Afternoon of the Sex Children', perfects the ideal of the privileged self by appealing to a notion of its 'truth' – the truth, that is, of 'what you already *were*'. The industry in self-improvement recognises youth's special status as the 'fundamental experience of a vanishing commodity, the ur-experience of obsolescence'. We are thus invited, as consumers, to think of ourselves as floating Theseus's Ships. Despite the transformations – both physical and spiritual – that ageing ought to bring, we're asked to imagine our bodies as eternally self-identical, to realise this ideal by buying back our youth.

Fantasies of endless renovation have a venerable history. In his *Metaphysics*, Aristotle advances a theory of change that answers precisely to the Theseus's Ship conundrum. For Aristotle, the kind of change figured by the plank-by-plank replacement of Theseus's Ship should be described as merely 'accidental'. Just as changes to a piece of wood's dampness are accidental to its fundamental woodiness, so can the basic parts of the ship be considered merely accidental to its association with Theseus.

'Essential' change to the vessel, by contrast, might follow from a change in its symbolic relationship to Theseus himself, or to the Greeks, whose greatness was woven by legend, if not by material process, into its very sails.

Through his notion of accidental change, Aristotle provides the tools with which to justify replacement as necessary to self-preservation. It also offers means of rationalising the absorption into that self of an Other. The crumple-necked woman's ovaries will be replaced by those of a monkey and yet, she believes, this will only make her outer appearance reflect more accurately the self she truly is.

Barthes observed this type of thinking – this privileging of the symbolic – to be little more than an agent of reproduction for capitalist society. He declared the modern world a system of infinite replacements, in which the fantasy of dominant identities is constructed not from matter, but from images and words endowed with the spurious magic of the essential.

Maggie Nelson's 2015 memoir *The Argonauts,* a well-known use of Theseus's Ship as a metaphor for selfhood, performs an emotional struggle to resist the essentialising impulse. On the one hand Nelson makes a commitment to refusing claims on fixed identity, and leverages the gender transition of her partner Harry Dodge to give this commitment context. On the other, she also both writes and lives by a desire for the kinds of reassuring absolutes that a ship that changes but 'remains the same' ultimately suggests. The conflict is intentional, Nelson's belief being that 'there is much to be learned from wanting something both ways'.

However, as Dodge approaches the process of hormone therapy, Nelson frets over its possible dangers, the ways in which it might change the person whose coherence has become her world. '*I feel like I can give you everything without giving myself away*', she whispers to him in bed, while wanting to be so comprehensively *his* as to agitate for the removal of tattoos that point to former lovers. Pregnant, she vows to let her baby know 'where the me and the non-me begin', as though to school him at the earliest moment in the fantasy of pure self-assertion. With each recurrence of the ship as a visualisation of the memoir's central tension, it is less the attachment to ambivalence and more the sentimental cleavage to a boundaried individual self that comes to dominate the page.

Theseus's Ship never offers more than an illusion of 'having it both ways'. If accepted as essentially fixed, the ship offers only a cursory gesture towards flux while shoring up the power of identity in all the senses that count. Where this limited notion of accidental change is allowed to stand in for 'progress' – without, that is, the need to accommodate radical upheaval – the political project of dissolving (in this case) the gender binary runs into inevitable trouble.

*

The valorisation of youth is merely one example of the wellness industry's endless calls to self-essentialisation. Another is a powerful psychology of selfhood that thwarts the most enlightened intentions. Common to these is a preoccupation with purity of the self, both spiritual and clinical in nature. The late artist Helen Chadwick's installation *Blood Hyphen*, first shown in 1988 but restaged and screened since, distils the electrifying force of introspection that medical technology can bring. The original piece involved projection of the artist's cervical cells directly onto the walls of a Clerkenwell chapel. Splashing this feat of microscopy across territory once reserved for the divine, *Blood Hyphen* is a secular monument to the scientific breakdown of barriers to 'looking inside' oneself.

Yet, perhaps on the basis of my own familiarity with regular cervical screenings – a phenomenal medical offering that can be anxiously loaded for the person screened – *Blood Hyphen* speaks to me less of godlike sophistication than of a troubling presence of the godly and pure in discourses on the feminised body. Here old values, typically the kind that discipline women and girls, infiltrate the scene of novelty in genuine medical progress.

In 1942, an Italian physician conducting a study on the prevalence of uterine cancer found the groups most free from disease to be virgins and nuns – an opportune basis for casting that illness into the shades of the corrupted.

When in 2006 the first licenses for vaccines protecting against human papillomavirus
(HPV) – the largely sexually transmitted virus
that causes most cases of cervical cancer – were
issued in the USA, HPV became a crucible
of angst around young girls' sexual activity,
whether protected and consensual or not. From
the Christian right there issued anti-vax lobbies;
from the centre there issued a gendered counter-
discourse in which mothers (not fathers) were
encouraged to vaccinate their daughters (but
never their sons). All seemed to ask that women
remain, on both a physical and spiritual level,
guardians of the boundaries that preserved their
inner 'selves' from outside contamination.

Cervical changes that warrant investigation
tend to suggest an unlikely but possible crawl
towards cancer rather than cancer itself. Doctors
and nurses will trace, over a period of years, the
progression of a set of cells, but intervention
is only necessary in cases of serious escalation.
The receptionist who booked me in for my
first biopsy reassured me that I should think of

these appointments as a matter of 'wellbeing' as opposed to a crisis of health.

Yet the language of wellness, however proper to this context, has proven in its larger context to be less a reassurance than an invitation to perpetual self-scrutiny. 'Don't even worry about it,' the doctor didn't say. When first I was shown the precancerous damage to my own cervical cells blown up into an abstraction on a hospital screen, the gynaecologist warned me that I ought to 'take heed' of the patio of 'crazy paving' covering the entrance to my womb. When I asked what this might mean in practice, he suggested, Rilke-like, that I had to change my life.

So as though on a spiritual cleanliness crusade and despite in some sense knowing better, I have found myself studying the progression of others' precancerous cells, intent on locating some key to the purification, the healthy replacement, of my own. Forums and blogs of this genre – at once communities of shame and valuable sites of solidarity – are littered with expressions not only of terror but deep remorse, meekly expressed among tips for outwitting HPV. Those who aren't in relationships retreat from the sexual field, as though to reassert the form of the self as the innocent, otherless child.

On these forums, we verse ourselves in the rudiments of the body's immune response while assuming personal responsibility for every operation of filtering, flushing, ingestion, deflation and destruction of which that immune response consists. We embrace daily exercise, drown in turmeric tea and attempt to 'think the virus away' with the assistance of apps that, for the download fee, promise the spiritual key to this and everything else on earth.

My last cigarette was on my twenty-sixth birthday, the day before I received the results of my first cervical smear. Quitting made my flesh feel like an overstrained bin bag yet nevertheless I struggled in my soul to feel sufficiently punished. Like a disapproving nun I instructed myself to estimate the number of times I had thus polluted my mouth. It was as though I might chant Hail Marys in an effort to cleanse the effects of the circa 30,000.

Vaccinated as I had in fact been thanks to both my parents, it seemed to me the fault for any viral damage would always be my own, having failed to abstain from the sexual act during which I presumably contracted it. Though tediously and suspiciously couched in the language of 'empowerment', narratives of purity were everywhere and had won the day by default. The nurse who was present at that first appointment reassured me it would have taken something like a 'full body condom' to avoid the moment of infection. This nevertheless prompted me to wonder if that would have been so hard.

*

In Ottessa Moshfegh's 2018 novel *My Year of Rest and Relaxation*, a young woman sets to plotting her own cellular transformation – a project of total overhaul she believes will change her life.

The book has been hailed by many as exemplary of a certain millennial affect. On a narrative level, it describes an affluent New Yorker's attempt to escape her own correctly identified anhedonia by means of a nonchalant scheme of self-purification. Having acquired a panoply of sedatives from an unscrupulous doctor, the unnamed narrator's plan is to restore herself to factory settings. The means by which she'll do this is through several months of enforced, continuous sleep: 'I knew in my heart', she explains, 'that when I'd slept enough, I'd be renewed, reborn. I would be a whole new person, every one of my cells regenerated enough times that the old cells were just distant, foggy memories'.

The narrator is depressed, disgusted even, by the mores of those with whom she surrounds herself – the awfulness of her jock boyfriend, the unattractive sensitivity of his hipster counterparts, and the insufferable neediness of Reva, her merely 'pretty' best friend ('an 8 out of 10 but ... a "New York 3"') even in contrast to the cold vacuity of beautiful New York women.

Acclimatised to her moneyed environment's furniture of selfishness and greed, the narrator can imagine no response to these problems beyond the boundaries of her own body. The rubric within which she attends to this body is that of the spiritual mission. She thinks of her private doctor, who suspects she might be FDA but prescribes her medications nonetheless, as a 'pharmaceutical shaman', and makes her payments to this 'sorcerer' into the kind of wooden box used in churches for candle donations.

Throughout the novel the narrator sustains an elegantly bilious tone. She is wise, for example, to the ambient disingenuity of the 'radical' New York art scene in which, in 'indecipherably cool avant-garde outfits', she pretends to make a living. She is quick, moreover, to mock the inanity of Reva's addiction to self-help. Yet cynicism towards a 'self-help society' fails to elevate the cynic above its structure of desire. Muffled between these critical barbs is a similar subjectivity – a credulous hope that the therapy provided by sleep will regenerate not only the cells inside her, but the very fabric of her world.

The narrator is surely aware that accumulated hours of sleep, much like accumulations of prescription drugs, offer no such marginal utility as commodified healthcare suggests. Health, unlike the ideal commodity, cannot be reduced to a quantified series of replaceable, exchangeable units any more than rebirth can be reduced to the replacement of cells. If we experience no diminishing returns as we multiply our prescriptions, it is because there will never be enough to take us to the state that we are seeking. The state we are seeking is not a question of 'enough', yet we want it with such force that we'll convince ourselves it is.

Herbert Marcuse argued that radical change requires the cultivation of desires that can't be fulfilled or accommodated by capitalist logics. By contrast, the impulses described by Moshfegh's narrator, while given in the language of transformation, simply reproduce the drive for infinite introspection. Rather than seeking to insert herself into systems of interdependence – developing friendships or networks of care beyond her bubble of disdain – the narrator is unable to exercise desire beyond the terms and objects provided by private healthcare. Her will, inasmuch as she has one, points less towards a different world than a recursive, narcotically softened simulation of the one in which she already lives.

For as long as this ideal of 'betterness' is confined to a horizon of self-improvement, the only desire-fulfilment involved is that of products and services. Thus the 'essential', irreplaceable self, subject to change only in the sense of 'accidental' malfunctions and improvements, becomes the site of fantasies of total replacement that regenerate and reproduce not flesh itself but, more significantly, the industry around it.

*

By the year 2000, in which *My Year of Rest and Relaxation* opens, the real-world market in 'cryobanking' as a self-preservation service was already emerging from the fringes of biotech and the realm of science-fiction into a mainstream Western market. Private companies preserving stem cells from cord blood, cord tissue and dental tooth pulp now offer this service to the wishful rich as a means of reconstructing themselves as their bodies wilt.

In their marketing copy, these companies draw attention to stem cells' capacity for self-renewal and differentiation, and therefore to their promise of being able to repair or replace damaged cells or tissues – to harness once again the material of *what you already were*. As the sociologist Nik Brown observes, within private biobanking, which connects its set of promises with emerging developments in tissue engineering, bone marrow transplantation and gene therapy, the client is shifted away from established therapeutic worlds and towards the future-oriented vision of regenerative medical economies.

Perhaps at the height of my anxieties I would have been tempted by the idea of returning to my own birth, a moment that one private cryobank describes as 'a once-in-a-lifetime opportunity to freeze a spare immune system'. There exist, however, no such means of gathering the past for future use, even for the superrich, to say nothing of the poor. 'Every cell is a kingdom of both substance and spirit', writes Anne Boyer in her memoir *The Undying* (2019), 'and every kingdom can be overthrown'. Describing the merciless effects of cancer on her body, Boyer insists that the 'lost parts of our souls are no more replaceable than the lost parts of our bodies, life incrementally lifting from life, just like that.' 'And there we are', she writes, 'mostly dead, but still required to go to work'.

While the rich go in search of their immortal selves, others must steer the great ship, fated to face the truth that it is they who are merely accidental. To the mind of the individual, Boyer notes, 'it should always be other people's faces that are swollen from steroids, not my own, not my own breasts gone now, replaced by glue and cold silicone'.

The suffering of others, of women, Boyer thinks, on flipping through third-person books about cancer, is generalised by this genre into literary opportunity – readable instalments of others' loss of self through which we might somehow avoid our own. Meanwhile the wellness economy's traffic in nebulous losses of self is generalised so fully as to ensnare even the mostly well. Narratives of age, impurity and sadness as failures of 'being oneself' ensure that even those who walk largely free from the burden of actual illness pour their financial resources into being *yet more alive.*

Despite my now mindlessly habitual dedication to a non-smoking, exercising life of supplement taking, the mildly threatening cells that are settled in my cervix have not, in their annual microscopic tribute to *Blood Hyphen*, shown signs of dramatic movement in any particular direction. I am under no illusion that this stillness represents the success of any magical thinking, neither concerning cell replacement nor, indeed, my 'self'. That line of thought, it seems to me on revisiting the adventure, is a crazy-paved path to delusions I would rather not reprise.

In 2012 the artists Revital Cohen and Tuur van Balen mounted an installation they called The Immortal – an assemblage of connected life-support machines that lived and breathed without recourse to any human flesh. In a choreographed loop of vital operations, salt water (a replacement for blood), oxygen and electrical impulses flowed through cords connecting the machines in one, self-sufficient closed circuit – Heart-Lung, Dialysis, Incubator, Ventilator, Cell Salvage Machine.

The Immortal deconstructed the notion of humans as collections of replaceable parts. Here we saw the reach for infinity of a hypothetical being blessed with unqualified access to medical intervention in its body. To perceive the body as a kind of replaceable machine, thought the artists, was a quintessentially Western trait, reliant on quantification. To how many 'beats per minute' can you reduce the idea of a heart? What social value must a heart possess to justify its clinical replacement – by parts with a specific cost attached to their production and use? Once the bulk of a human body has been replaced, how much further can it reasonably go towards defending the self's immortality? Where are the edges of possible commitment to an irreplaceable self when the self insists on its own reduction to a jumble of replaceable parts?

Among the machines assembled here as essential to organic life, one in particular stands out. The Intraoperative Cell Salvage Device is designed for exceptional cases (frequently religious) where a patient might refuse to take a blood transfusion from a person other than themselves. The device allows the recipient's blood, collected at the site of operation, to be processed and returned to recipient's own veins. If such a machine seems surplus to basic life support, it was, however, essential to the work's ironic force. For the tangle of 'foreign' bodies made of stainless steel and wood belied the Western delusion that a self can survive without external intervention. The only way to sustain the illusion of a pure, immortal self is to inhabit this contradiction.

In her book *On Immunity*, Eula Biss deconstructs how obsessions with purity and self-sufficiency produce an approach to health that ends up harming the majority. Biss observes that, despite the debunking of scientific literature cited by the anti-vax movement, liberal middle-class parents continue to shun vaccination. In 2014, the year of the book's publication, the US had seen a resurgence of mumps, whooping cough and measles – seemingly antiquated infections revived by individualistic sentiment. Concerned with dispelling the delusion that public health is independent of the private, the book makes the case for recognising bodies as vitally interdependent.

The fixation on personal purity that Biss identifies does violence across gender, sex-uality, class and race. Anti-sodomy laws, the sterilisation of working-class women and the vaccination of smallpox-era Black Americans at gunpoint attest to the rootedness of medicalised fear in mistrust of those considered 'other'. Yet given the actual physical dependency of those in power on those they systematically oppress, their invocations of 'physical protection' stand on tremulous ground.

One of the first successful human-to-human heart transplants took place in South Africa in 1967 and involved the replacement of a European Jewish man's heart with the heart of Clive Haupt – a dead man designated legally as 'coloured'. This life-saving merging of bodies was celebrated even by supporters of Apartheid, a system grounded in myths that white self-protection required segregation. How would they justify such a concession to the falsity of their beliefs?

As a member of the Nationalist party then put it, 'The heart is merely a blood-pumping machine and whether it comes from a white, black or coloured man – or a baboon or a giraffe for that matter – has no relevance to the issue of race relations in the political or ideological context'. Black body parts, while treated as essential to the maintenance and survival of white ones, were at the same time constructed as merely 'accidental' to a watertight white identity. For as long as, in wider society, the use of Black subjects resembled the function of timbers on Theseus's Ship – throwaway parts of a national vessel whose sail was officially white – so would their bodies be similarly imagined, pronounced and handled.

Organ donation, like vaccination, is a system fundamental to a society's immunitary health. As a community-based system, it protects not only individuals, but also the broader society in which it is embedded. As such, despite its functional distinctness from medical immunisation, organ donation can be thought of as 'immunitary' in a broader, political sense.

By this logic the nation-state is also an immune system, as is the village, the household or the law. Indeed, as the political philosopher Robert Esposito reminds us, 'immunity' was first of all a political category – the pivot, he suggests, around which our entire symbolic universe revolves.

In any immunitary unit, the community agrees to partake in a collective system of protection. *Munus* in Latin refers to a gift or provision, but also a duty or obligation. A properly functioning community depends on a willingness to give as well as take, a subject's entitlement to gifts depending on their fulfilment of duties. The entitlements and commitments around which a community (*communitas*) is built are mutually assured by those involved through generalised participation.

When thinking in immunitary terms, it is not hard to see how the arrangement of social formations by borders and separations comes to be framed as a necessary feature of protection. Defensive postures against invasion by a body constructed as foreign appear simply to mirror the body's immune response to a pathogen.

Yet the last fifty years have seen a drastic increase, within industrialised societies, in cases of autoimmune disease – conditions in which the body mistakes its own cells for foreign agents and stages an assault on itself. In an essay titled 'How to Be A Person in the Age of Autoimmunity', the artist and writer Carolyn Lazard, herself subject to this form of affliction, describes a situation of 'constant fatigue and discomfort punctuated by brief, high dramas of flares and successive hospitalizations'. Such also is the fate of violently divided Western nations, whose immunitary divisions transgress what any notion of a 'commons' can support.

In contexts where divisions between self and other give on to systemic exploitation, *im*munity for those on the side of power takes the form of an exemption from duty. Such exemption invariably places a heavier burden on the powerless. According to Esposito, members of this disempowered class are not immune, but rather *de*mune. The demunised subject lives in a worst-of-both-worlds – obliged to give to the community that refuses them its protections.

The immune are the immortal gods serviced by gold-spun robots; they are the heroes of states whose fleets are propelled by acts of human sacrifice. They are those with access to vaccination from sexually transmitted viruses, or Helen DeWitt's elaborately satisfied middle managers. *Lightning Rods* is a tale about the demunised subjects whose replaceable labour underpins corporate man's immunitary construction of his 'self'.

Concerns around replacement in the work-force, and even in personal relations, frequently converge around a sense of some likely material threat. As the threat of replacement is internalised, however, fear becomes existential – as nebulous as it is total – and seems to struggle to locate it's object. 'They will not replace us' was the chant that haunted 'Unite the Right' rallies in Charlottesville in 2017, the anonymity of 'they' attesting to the malleability of imagined hazards to the self.

In 2011, far-right confabulist Jean Renaud Gabriel Camus published a book that theorised his suspicion of a so-called *Great Replacement*. By 2017 the theory had gathered a horrifying weight of influence, with YouTube channels, Gab and 8chan accounts dedicated solely to diverse formulations of its racial replacement theory. Camus's particular line had been that France's 'indigenous' white population was being subjected to a pernicious process of replacement by stealth invasion.

His chosen pathogens were Arab, North African and Sub-Saharan Muslim populations. This process of replacement, Camus proposed, had been midwifed by a group of 'replacist elites', led in their miscegenating ways by the European Union. In the US, similar charges have since been levelled at Jewish, Muslim and Mexican-American targets, inspiring multiple shootings in synagogues and mosques.

Scooping out paranoid corners of the mind and mushing them together on forums, proponents of Great Replacement discourse have enjoyed a degree of mainstream acceptance. Following the Christchurch mosque shooting in 2019, the BBC invited a nationalist pundit onto Newsnight for 'expert' comment. In 2020, LBC encouraged a white supremacist, who'd attempted to call in on one of their previous shows to propose an ethno-state policy, to call in again and speak her mind to the Labour Party leader. 'Should white people start playing identity politics', the woman asked Starmer, 'before they become a minority themselves by 2066? Why couldn't she, as an 'indigenous' white British citizen, have such exclusive rights of self-determination as are given to citizens of Israel? 'We all have those rights', came Starmer's mealy mouthed response, before moving on unruffled, affirming the caller's identity game as already somewhat successful.

Camus's contextualisation of his thesis in a broader suspicion of Brussels renders its successes comparable with those of UKIP. Having long been a fringe presence, UKIP finally found its fanbase as the Great Replacement

theory was first seeping through cyberspace –
a time when the Conservative leadership were
stirring pots of anti-immigration venom while
failing to deliver on their promised response.
UKIP proved successful in appealing to thwarted
desires for stricter control on immigration, while
selling its anti-immigrant line under the more
respectable banner of 'Euro-scepticism'. Thus its
supporters found a willing ear for their ethno-
centric line without being asked to surrender
their identification as 'not racist'.

The 'activists' of Isabel Waidner's 2019 novel
We Are Made of Diamond Stuff are first seen
attempting to explain their xenophobia by
wielding the rainbow flag. Looking 'like Justin
Bieber, only paler', they won't let 'bigots' enter
their country. They stand against a so-called
'homophobic Islam' and think that Muslim
culture is incompatible with Western ideas.
'They're not racist (they say), they're *progressive*'.
    Territorial over the boundaries of their own
difference, the Bieber lookalikes hold multiple

hostilities towards the novel's two queer protagonists – both of them second-generation economic
migrants. The Biebers believe that the queerness
of this pair brings gayness into disrepute.

Yet Waidner is careful to emphasise that
the Biebers have been subject to the influence
of years of Conservative governance – of a
divide-and-rule agenda that creates the illusion
that they themselves (as sexual minorities,
members of the white working class) constitute
the origin of hatred. Indeed, as robot solidarity
gathers devastating pace in the third act of
R. U. R., the surviving humans lament not having given the robots national identities. If only
they had set up factories in every state – each to
make robots of a different colour, language and
factory mark – then power to control society
might have stayed just where it was. 'How
many times can you divide a minority culture?'
Waidner's protagonists wonder.

As the narrative *of Diamond Stuff* develops,
we witness the Biebers' transition from UKIP
and the EDL into the political mainstream,

where they find larger platforms from which to espouse the anti-immigrant word. 'Better career options', the narrator comments – 'they might go into politics professionally'.

The fantasy of having options where there are none, anchored in a hope for a future less characterised by threat – this conforms to what Lauren Berlant describes as 'cruel optimism' in her 2011 book of that name. Optimism is cruel, says Berlant, for those without control over the material conditions of their lives. For such subjects, the relation to a fantasy that their own private fate is at one with the fate of the nation – a nation that promises to become great again – can be all that psychically protects them from being destroyed.

Yet what is particularly cruel about this optimism is its self-sabotaging nature; the way in which the object of the subject's desire is in fact a hindrance to their flourishing. Xenophobia offers us a classic example: an autoimmune hostility to Others without whom there would be no 'nation' to protect.

The characters who populate *Diamond Stuff* seek to wrest control of their lives by ever evolving means, yet never progress beyond different permutations of their own precarity. 'Where's reality? I want to change it', one protagonist gasps, printer ink bleeding from the flimsy blue cardboard of their permanent residence card.

*

Before the development of vaccines, the Anglo-American response to Covid-19 was notable for both its immunitary weakness and autoimmune malfunction. Death rates clustered disproportionately among people of colour: Black women were more than twice as likely to die as white.

The demunised were sloughed off through low living standards and occupational exposure; the country's immunised gods learned musical instruments and worked from home. A migrant workforce of carers and cleaners, delivery and transport workers – many of them casual workers without sick pay or adequate protection – laboured to produce the 'immunity' enjoyed by the middle classes, all the while remaining at the mercy of a hostile environment and No Recourse to Public Funds.

These, however, the voice of Britain boomed through the pestilent air, were times that called for *community*. As webs of police tape were spun around park benches (sitting an activity now strictly for home), civic-minded townspeople gathered round their phones to set up forums for 'mutual aid'.

Within those first peculiar months of lockdown, I bore unprecedented witness to the souls of my immediate neighbours as they embraced each other with a formerly unthinkable intimacy. Yet while I was impressed by their sharing of knowledge on the whereabouts of flour, not to mention the escalating local price of milk, there was surely something rather limited in this conception of the mutual.

'Can we please report random people social-ising outside local businesses', is one of Carol's first suggestions for mutual caregiving. As the neighbourhood chat gathers momentum, these 'local businesses' are identified as three nearby Portuguese cafés, their patrons drawn from the large community that has been known as Little Portugal since the 1960s, when South London served as a place of refuge from political violence.

'Are these idiots on a different planet?' Simon asks. 'Police, get on our streets and patrol!' Anne wonders if 'perhaps they have only been tuning into the Madeiran news'. Carol again: 'They have no reason to be hanging around our streets.' Infectious standers-round and queuers-up for Easter pastries, 'they' are cast as at once vectors for the virus and viral invaders themselves.

The striking consistency, over the months, of the group's xenophobic repartee was mirr-ored in its starkly exclusionary geographic conception. Limited in range to two rows of Victorian terraces, excluding the hundreds of council flats that separated these, its topography was less like a simulation of communal life than a digital accretion of enclosed back yards. The philosopher Peter Sloterdijk describes the private dwelling as the place in which immunitary fantasy finds its best physical support. Man, holed up in his 'ignoring machine', thereby physically interiorises his sense of his own protection. 'Toxic people', Sloterdijk writes, 'must stay outside, and bad news too if possible'.

Mere weeks into the US's acknowledgement of crisis, the then-President had moved to announce the following immunitary measure:

In light of the attack from the Invisible Enemy, as well as the need to protect the jobs of our GREAT American Citizens, I will be signing an Executive Order to temporarily suspend immigration to the United States.

Stephen Miller, one of its authors, was reported to have proclaimed in a conference call the belief that 'Americans of every political stripe' would rally behind the initiative. 'Those individuals have a right and an expectation', he supposed, 'to get their jobs back and not to be replaced by foreign workers'. This, he concluded, was a 'historic' act.

If such an act was historic, it seems remarkably consistent with pre-existing conditions. Aligning the tendencies of 'foreign' bodies with the virus's aptitude for invasion, the order was a tidy summary of the established immunitary discourse: immigrant as public liability; border as cutaneous protection.

The relative replaceability of demonised foreign workers has furthermore long been a strategy for expanding exploitation's parameters. Threats of dismissal and of deportation for both documented and undocumented migrants force the acceptance of ever more undignified conditions and sub-legal pay. In swift recognition of the order's likely autoimmune effects – the presence of immigrant labour being essential to pandemic-control – its terms were swiftly amended to allow for a number of exceptions; medical and agricultural workers would still be allowed to 'invade'.

By the time the US was burning over racist police brutality and protests began to erupt around our South London enclave, you might have thought the exchange of tips for snitching on 'random' others to the Met would have come to seem a little uncouth.

Yet as Andrew traded his last few issues of the *TLS* for Simon's stack of *Private Eye*s, and as Lynn gifted her surplus Abel and Cole purple potatoes to a suitably delighted neighbour, Alan joined the discussion to express support for a new pro-surveillance petition and con-fusion at protestors outside. Maria says they're headed towards the American embassy. She tentatively adds that she might join. 'We are not part of America?????' comes Alan's thunderous response, as though the recent shock of perceiving solidarity has genuinely made him unsure. As outbursts of grief in the United States echo off the pavement outside, the residents of Little Portugal are united in one belief: that an alcohol license for a certain local café is the 'worst thing they can possibly imagine'.

The demunised need not be deported to experience daily exclusion from a country's immunitary formations. 'The father's house may have many rooms', as Sloterdijk puts it, 'but the high price ensures that most of them are empty.' When the longed-for police did eventually appear within our midst that summer, it was in haste, to the scene of an actual crime on one of the neighbouring estates. In a flat where 'too many people' were later reported to have been living, a South American couple had been stabbed in the middle of a lockdown afternoon. 'Disgraceful', Carol was promptly moved to comment. 'Lockdown may be inconvenient but does not excuse stabbing people'.

*

Eula Biss's genealogy of fear when it comes to vaccination converges upon the 'longstanding belief that disease is a product of those we define as others'. Her argument for vaccination as a means to 'herd immunity' might seem counterintuitive 'if we think of our bodies as inherently disconnected from other bodies'. 'Which, of course', she adds, 'we do'.

In the sincerity of this 'of course', Biss betrays a sensibility that perhaps explains the discomfort she feels, despite her book's good intentions, with adopting the language of the 'herd'. Its suggestion of cattle awaiting death, its gesture towards pack mentality, jars with her unbreakable commitment to individual freedom. She offers that, instead, we might prefer to think of a hive of bees – 'matriarchal, environmental do-gooders who also happen to be entirely interdependent'.

A resistance to interdependence haunts the best of liberal intentions – a refusal to allow it to be more than an accidental feature of a world where the individual remains sovereign. Biss holds back from proposing that the herd might itself be a desirable formation. Cataloguing evidence for the rootedness of 'our' fears, she characterises individualist self-protection as part of a 'behavioural immune system' described by evolutionary psychologists, as though some inflexible 'human nature' determined possible thought. 'There will always', she writes, 'be diseases against which we cannot protect ourselves, and those diseases will always tempt us to project our fears onto other people'.

The belief that, for long as disease exists, human relations will always absorb an excess of immunitary logic speaks to the limits that neoliberal thought has placed on imagination. Vaccination has indeed been the best defence against Covid-19, one that doesn't depend upon the sacrifice of demunised subjects. And yet, as the now-ubiquitous term 'vaccine nationalism' suggests, mere consent to a jab within one's (local, national) immune unit leaves untouched the power relations that designate sacrificial victims. Vaccination can certainly be an act of community. Community, however, is defined by more than defence against a single virus.

In an essay responding to the European migrant crisis of 2015, Paul B. Preciado observes that the psychology of national exceptionalism is related to the notion of identity as quantifiable object. The 'self' in this formation is a site to be enlarged and protected, pitted against its Other in a universe of threatened replacements. It is this quality of ego-construction, Preciado writes, that leads each actor on the world's stage, no matter what disaster results, to 'affirm his, her or their role in the scene as real, authentic and irreplaceable'. To deviate from the ending to which this script leads requires, he suggests, the daunting task of 'Forgetting the Idea of Being Special'.

Fear of disease and desire for protection can easily lead to dismissal of others as disposable, just as fear of replacement can lead to assertions of the individual self as uniquely worthy of preservation. Easily, however, is not the same as necessarily. Esposito writes that the self-destructive phenomenon of autoimmunity occurs when immunitary logic is stretched too far. With regard to Covid-19, he notes that this 'threshold is crossed exactly when social distancing demands a total rupture of social bonds'. Could social distancing be said to have *demanded* from my neighbours the rejection of their own community members?

The awareness of one's own replaceability that is raised by an imagined threat can arc into a cruelly optimistic identification with the irreplaceable – a figure who exists entirely for the preservation of himself. It is possible, however, that those who are made replaceable by society can, in consciousness of their misuse, identify instead as a class. While Alan was scoffing into his phone about our distance from American grief, less than a mile away, thousands had assembled to demonstrate and march. 'Distanced' enough from each other to stretch beyond visible range, all these people were nevertheless arranged as a single mass.

Replace Me! In 2011 the artist Rosemarie Trockel used this command to name a sculptural installation consisting of two identical sofas – full-sized ceramic lozenges sheathed in a plastic sheet. The plaster-cast sculpture had been vitrified, a process that tames amorphous masses into rigid, concentrated forms.

As though existing in conflict with its precision manufacturing, *Replace Me* stands defiant against Forgetting the Idea of Being Special. We are called on to witness the betrayal contained in this counterfeit sofa padding, soft as a human heart until it turns out to be hard, the hardness of clay replaceable by infinite further hardness. The '*Me*' of the title's provocation suggests an individual scorned – someone who, like most, supposes themselves above replacement. Draped on the machine-made sculpture is a mess of woollen blanket.

Thrown into unrepeatable folds on its bed of uniform plastic, the blanket looks like a trace of the special one, the artist. 'Replace me', in the context of this work, is both an invitation and an accusation – a trap, an alluring dare.

'One day you make love to a replacement, having finally bedded the person you loved', goes a line from the poet Adam Fitzgerald's *The Lordly Hudson*. 'And before / long, replacement you lounges with replacement them / on a green sofa that is a fine forgery of itself'.

Can there be a 'replacement them' without this implying a replacement you? These sentimental sofas of artist and poet seem to dramatise a psychic impasse: the individual wants to be free to make his own replacements, but cannot accept the possible application to himself.

In 1923 a Parisian woman referred to as *Mme M* became a subject of intrigue in medical research. A psychiatrist named Joseph Capgras had reported how, shortly following the loss of two daughters and twin boys, *Mme M* succumbed to the unshakeable belief that her one remaining daughter and, subsequently, her husband had been (respectively) kidnapped and murdered and replaced by identical imposters.

Capgras syndrome, as it is now known, is a rare but strangely familiar-sounding psychiatric disorder in which the sufferer believes that one or more people have somehow been replaced by doubles. It seems the imposter most often stands in for someone close to the subject – typically a sexual partner, or sometimes a family member. Sometimes, indeed, the imposter replaces the subject of delusion herself.

That Capgras syndrome has been identified as a problem not of misrecognition but rather of misbelief perhaps explains why it has often been subjected to psychodynamic analysis rather than sciences of perception. For Freud it seemed clear that 'replacement me' was coextensive with 'replacement them'. Our very selves, he thought, were formed in the dregs of those we have loved and lost – the mother who feeds, the man who protects and their infinite replacements. Each love object in the course of a life is a replacement for the first. Each of these is internalised such that grief – an emptying out of the world – transmutes into an emptied out self.

If transference, the displacement of unfinished love onto endless substitute persons, represents, for Freud, a cornerstone of human emotional life, then narcissism – another of his signal concepts – explains why this brings such pain. We are all, he thought, narcissists, whose autoerotic desires are bound with an instinct to survive. The current object of affection, then, not only stands in for the original, but also for your sense of self – your idea of who *you* once were, or your future ego ideal. In every *replacement them* you retrieve the sense of a special *me*, yet each represents the likelihood that you too are someone's replacement.

Freudian ideas are somewhat at odds with most romantic ideals, to which even those of us with cynical proclivities often find ourselves attached. I once had a boyfriend with whom I tried to defy the possessive investment that defines the narcissistic lover, joining the many among whom the attempt at liberation takes the form of the 'open relationship'.

The experience itself was less one of freedom than 'openness' implies. Acknowledging each other's extramarital dates with an air of casual acceptance, we seethed at one another in our every word. In bed, across the bath, at family events and in photos where we'd grimace side by side, we'd spatially assert our togetherness while hating each other's guts. You needn't, it turns out, look kindly on a person to want to stake claims on their existence. Love doesn't always successfully motivate 'letting someone go'.

While performing a degree of consent to my own eventual replacement I had nevertheless failed to imagine that its agent could be as 'real' as myself. I imagined she would function to my boyfriend as superficially as a replacement eye. Projecting, that is, a semblance of bodily wholeness to onlookers while offering nothing of the eye's original function. I thought of this

intruder like a skin graft, a thing of unmistak-
able distortion, destined always to signal what
had been there before. And yet, she seemed to
surface entirely whole, slicing through any such
delusions. Younger and less embittered than me,
her skin looked perfectly smooth.

Had it once been me who'd taken the position
of smooth-skinned replacement? Was this about
to be me again wherever I went next? Empty
gestures of private dissent from normative
romantic relations had failed to prevent any
tendency to ruminate on questions such as
these. Acts of political 'lifestyle', indifferent to
the lives of others, weren't, it seemed, going to
save me from vanity or pride.

Early studies of Capgras syndrome found that
when the belief is in a double of the self, the
patient asserts that imposters in her image are
ruining her reputation. Or stealing the wealth
and property she has spent her life amassing –
taking what is rightfully hers. The threat here
seems less to metaphysical questions of 'reality'
or 'truth' than to socially contingent notions of

competitive status – notions of personal match-lessness that are violated by replacement.

Visions of replacements as interlopers – substitutes either for fetishised others or naturally special selves – may well resemble psychoanalytic pathologies. Nonetheless they are clearly conditioned by elements of social context. Workers are threatened with repla-cement to motivate them to compete, to assume responsibility for their compromised conditions of existence. Citizens are promised protection should they manage to achieve their best selves; should they manage to accumulate such wealth and power as to buy themselves exemption from the rule.

Buy yourself a younger body, hack yourself a purified soul, use the replacements available and avoid replacement yourself. Hang on to the job that is cancelling your joy or someone else will rise to the privilege. Cling to the boyfriend you have won for yourself (or pretend to be above this) – or else, farewell to any shreds of self-possession. It is a telling feature of this condition that the Capgras patient who believes that they themselves have been replaced often shows conviction that the 'real me' has died.

In an essay from 2008, Chris Kraus describes the 'insurmountable' challenges posed to her by the loss from her house of a black plastic scoop she had used to measure ground coffee. Starbucks no longer sold the coffee pots to which the scoop had been attached, having replaced them at some point with travel mugs. Kraus wonders, '*Just how much time and care should a person spend in the attempt to replace a fetishised object?* Or rather – does a commonplace object that, in its absence and newly unattainable state, *become* fetishised?'

When her ex-husband points out that this kind of desire, transferred onto an object, in fact defines the term fetish, Kraus protests that there is no 'Freudian guesswork' involved in her need for the scoop. And yet, she later wonders, might her need to recover the scoop be nothing more than self-affirmation – a claim, more than anything, to knowing what she wants?

Without the scoop's absorption into Kraus's sense of self, would it not have been possible to use a spoon or a different measuring item, without being so undone by the concession to loss? This seems to me a bit like asking, could my former boyfriend and I have *simply not* been narcissists. We, like Kraus, knew what it was that what we wanted, and it wasn't what we wanted to want. Wanting to want to transcend one's petty jealousies is not the same as actually transcending them.

Nothing in the world we had been formed in had trained us to desire in other ways, and desire is not reconfigured within the smallness of a couple's world. Perhaps, then, it is worth asking what kind of larger world it would be in which 'replace me' could lose its sting. In what kind of world might we *want* to transcend love's exceptionalising definition? Through what kinds of actions might we bring about the will to live in other ways?

*

No radical shift in desire was ever borne of a personal choice, nor out of any battle that simply asserts an individual right. When the Macaulay Company of publishing professionals took to the picket lines in 1934, it was more than a mere accumulation of private dispossessions that had broken their middle-class manners. As *New Masses* reported at the time, what brought the Macaulay staff to the height of their militancy was a structure of feeling that emerged *between* the employees rather than merely *within* them.

The 'distinctive feature of the strike', according to *New Masses*, was the expression of solidarity that flowed between workers – workers from other publishers but also bookshops, office workers sent by the union, journalists and authors. This dynamic confounded employers, who had failed to imagine that the desires of the class-conscious worker might not be limited to guarding his 'place' nor indeed to his own self-interest. The strikers had been moved to fight not only for their own eroded rights but notably in solidarity with Dorothy Rimmer – a union representative constructively dismissed for her moves towards organising colleagues. The strike was a rejection, in universal terms, of replacement's weaponisation.

At the start of 2020 I joined a strike with colleagues who, like me, worked in publishing. The strike was not, however, a publishing-specific event. Indeed the dissenting academics in whose institution our publishing projects were embedded enjoyed such healthy salaries as might make an editor squeal. In terms, however, of the casualised contracts endemic to this setting, the situation was notably worthy of dissent.

People I met on the picket line had dedicated decades of service to a college that continued to pay them by the (never guaranteed) hour. 'Hour' was something of a stand-in here for the several hours worked for each one paid, and payment for these hours carried with it only the most meagre of protections and benefits. Those who enjoyed what relative stability was on offer could broadly be predicted by gender and race. The relation between these and one's replaceability followed the trends established in Homer.

Those represented by a union are unlikely to share universal conditions, yet such conditions are not the concern of those whose desire is shaped by a group. To those of us emerging from an unsuccessful winter of toe-swelling daily canvassing, the emotional pull of the picket was recognised as greater than the sum of its pleasures. Weeks of lost earnings and ritual disdain from warm, dry picket-crossing colleagues are motivated not by innate desire but engulfment in collective commitment. To visions of something beyond the ugly mundanity of exploitation; to harnessing the strength in numbers that undoes capitalist realist torpor. The ego ideal to which you aspire when wedging yourself in a struggle comes not from gazing lovelorn upon your own reflection, but rather from managing to witness yourself through the eyes of others.

The political figure of the comrade exemplifies the struggle to Forget the Idea of Being Special, and in doing so transcends their learned sense of powerlessness. As the theorist Jodi Dean describes it, comradeship 'requires the dissolution of attachments to the fantasy of self-sufficiency, hierarchy and individual uniqueness'. It is a relation characterised by sameness and equality in the struggle towards communist life; a relation that exists when ideals are formed not through the ego, but collectively.

The comrade, writes Dean, is 'multiple, replaceable, fungible' – all that we've have been taught to fear. Yet if communism names the alternative to a capitalist order that cultivates competitiveness, self-interest and anxiety, comradeship must name a relation in which fear of replacement, and cruelly optimistic fantasies of an irreplaceable self, have no possible part. To resist the use of replaceability as a weapon of exploitation must entail its reassertion on alternative terms. The assertion, that is, of a replaceable self as radically equal to others, rather than radically vulnerable to capitalists' misuse.

Solidaristic assertions of equality in struggle might be seen as attempts to violate the divisions wrought by capitalism. Dean writes of the comrade's interchangeability as like that of the puppet, the cog or the robot inasmuch as it crucially arises not from whom one is, but from what is being done, since for as long as 'robots' – forced labourers – are subordinated to the contrivances of the capitalist class, lines will be drawn between them (*in colour, in language, in factory mark*) that differentiate what they can do. Joining in a common struggle subverts the intentions of this dynamic, using the exposure of difference as a weapon against division. 'White comrades to the front' was an important injunction in the summer of 2020, commanding that those whose replaceability tended to be least exploited make themselves most vulnerable in the common fight against differential oppression.

In a series of actions among culture workers that took place in London during the summer and autumn of 2020, workers sought to disgrace those Theseus's ships from which replaceable staff, for their efforts, were being thrown overboard. Workers raged as one with comrades from multiple unions against the use of their varying precarities – replaceability sliding into redundancy – in misconceived managerial strategies for saving their sinking vessels.

In 2017, outsourced workers at Tate, many of them on zero-hours contracts and less than living wages, had drawn the attention of unions after being asked to contribute to the cost of a boat for the gallery's outgoing director. In 2020, a £7 million bailout for Tate was promptly funnelled into the maintenance of 'essential' six-figure salaries, rather than saving 'commercial arm' jobs from total disappearance. Despite the ironic pandemic-era rebrand of 'accidental' workers as 'essential', orthodoxy remained blind, it seemed, to the importance of an arm to a body. The workers of Tate Enterprises, buoyed by solidarity from artists, public figures, and many more workers than those whose jobs were on the line, finally went on a strike that lasted forty-two days.

'I've never been able to answer to the word *comrade*', writes Maggie Nelson in *The Argonauts*, 'nor share in [its] fantasy of attack'. She writes this in the context of a defence of her decision to marry Harry – then legally 'female' – in haste before the passing in 2008 of California's Proposition 8. Proposition 8 would re-introduce the ban on 'same-sex' marriage.

Nelson is aware of marriage's flaws as a heteronormative, patriarchal, property-protecting institution. She recognises that the anti-assimilationist, 'comradely' stance might be ambivalence around fighting for the right to participate in such an arrangement. Yet here, she seems to suggest, love and politics essentially conflict. Framing the idea of politicised love as little more than a fetish, she imagines her dismissal of the banner-waving comrades: '*Our diagnosis is similar but our perversities are not compatible*'.

Comparison of comrades to robots and cogs who'd abandon their lovers for the cause understandably grates for those raised on fantasies of normative romance. Yet what if we think of the shape of love beyond this common construction, which anchors a certain kind of coupledom in a neutral, value-free magic?

'The principle which ought to be the guide of men who want to live nobly', Phaedrus famously declares in Plato's *Symposium*, is 'neither kindred, nor honour, nor wealth, nor any other motive as much as love'. The people we seek to become, he thinks, in the eyes of our lovers are the best and most honourable of all, for a person engaged in a dishonourable act 'will be more pained at being detected by his lover than anyone else'. Even the smallest army, he says, were it to be made of lovers, 'would surely overcome the world'.

'My God!' says Sarah Gordon to Vivian Gornick in *The Romance of American Communism*, an oral history of precisely what the title suggests, and its downfall in 1956. 'How I hated selling the *Worker*! I used to stand in front of the neighborhood movie on Saturday night with sickness and terror in my heart . . .

And then canvassing! Another horror.' 'But I did it', she goes on, 'I did it because if I didn't do it I couldn't face my comrades the next day'. If they didn't, as she puts it, 'push down the gagging' and go out to engage in political action, they'd suffer from the unbearable weight of the betrayal. Is this not a description of love as Phaedrus, via Plato, would have it?

In her essay 'Make Way for Winged Eros' (1923), the Bolshevik politician and thinker Alexandra Kollontai argued that, while it would not have been expedient to prioritise love on the eve of the Russian revolution, the world-building efforts of the years to follow would depend on its animating force.

Kollontai wrote that love, like any other psychological or social phenomenon, was a power whose strength could be just as dangerous to conservatism as to the left. Even romantic love between couples, rather than being an end in itself, could be turned outwards to enmesh with 'friendship, passion, maternal tenderness, sympathy, admiration and many other shades of emotion' – all means to the recognition of others' integrity and rights. For Kollontai, the 'perversities' of comradeship and love were by no means incompatible. Love could in fact be a communistic force, not just its egoistic opposite.

In *Love's Work* (1995) the late philosopher Gillian Rose, like Kollontai a Marxist, turns her wisdom and analytic powers on her own life's experiences to chart, through a series of episodes, both the promise of love as a political force and its limits within her own lifetime. Of her childhood adoration for the singer Roy Rogers, she notes that her desire for him had been inseparable from her unshakeable desire to *be* and to *have* him. She recalls her early idealisation of men as a Freudian gesture of paternal replacement, and describes on her sixteenth birthday changing her surname by deed poll from her father's to her stepfather's – an act of familial replacement and 'violent self-assertion'.

Rose's application of a left critique to her younger, inexperienced self is turned in her adult years upon the liberals who surround her. She cites the kind of 'cultured and idealising fantasy' that motivates flamboyant lonely-hearts ads in the *New York Review of Books* – the kind that turns against the dreamer to reinforce their terminal solitude. Behind fantasies of finding The One lies an ego ideal that dooms the lover to Freudian repetition, a cruel optimism that the Other will restore us to ourselves.

Kollontai's love demands the killing of such sacred cows. It is distinct from the established pattern in which a lover is given 'the right to the absolute and indivisible possession of the beloved person'. It is a question of subordinating Winged Eros – that fleeting but intoxicating passion – to the shadowy, swarming, long-term potential of 'love-duty to the collective'. This act of subordination is not one decision but a process of struggle, and yet, Kollontai believes, it would be wrong to lament this. Just as it is only through intentional acts of equality in struggle that we start to remake ourselves as equal, it is only through action that love can recreate itself too. First it must be practiced as an equalising force and, second, one that we desire. 'The new class', Kollontai writes, will be 'capable of developing new facets of emotion which possess unprecedented beauty, strength and radiance. As the cultural and economic base of humanity changes, so will love be transformed'.

While Rose is sceptical of any idea of total escape from the ego, she does suggest that there remains in this life the potential for transformation – a radical, processual reconception of the self as made in relation to others. On the cusp of her own untimely death, Rose discerns an enlightened subjectivity in the ninety-three-year-old figure of Edna, with whom she stays on a visit to New York. Rose observes that Edna exudes wellbeing precisely for not having lived a perfected life. 'She has not', she writes, been *exceptional*. 'She has not loved herself or others unconditionally'.

Rose learns from Edna a way of being, of re-
linquishing claims on unadulterated wholeness,
that rhymes with a certain serenity in relation
the body. Edna's most prominent feature, having recently contracted cancer of the face, is a
large prosthetic nose – a replacement to which,
without aspirations to sustaining an appearance
of 'herself', Edna is somewhat indifferent. In the
mornings she asks Rose if she would mind if
the nose were to remain unworn.

Faced with her own cancer and the change
it forces upon her, Rose becomes similarly
circumspect about the relation of her colostomy
– a 'surrogate rectum and anus' – to the self she
is expected to project. 'Deep brown, burnished
shit is extruded from bright, proud infoliation
in a steady paste-lime stream in front of
you', she writes. The colostomy separates the
act of excretion from its associated site of
pleasure and pain. To consider this would-be
replacement, she insists, 'is to describe a new
bodily function, not to redescribe the old'. Rose
shuns the distinction between 'accidental' parts

that make no difference to the whole, and those that express some 'essential' self; the colostomy, she insists, has nothing to do with 'imaginary self-representation'.

Rose is prepared to stare directly at the transmutation of her body without succumbing to fantasies of its eternal renewable sameness, its containment of any truth or essence of the soul. Likewise, in love there is porousness, incompleteness and decline. Her understanding of love is derived from an understanding of the self as one that that knows its vulnerabilities, defying the 'essential' status that sustains the glory of Theseus's Ship. Her understanding of love is unlike Nelson's enchantment with a vision of unbreachable connection or a truth of the self that, despite all acts of replacement, manages to endure.

For Nelson the image of Theseus's Ship suggests (after Barthes) how the phrase 'I love you' holds its shape even as it takes on new inflections with every utterance. For Rose, love is instead both vulnerable to destruction and loaded with potential for change. Not only change in relation to itself, but also in relation to the world. 'Love', as Kollontai wrote, 'is an emotion that unites, and is consequently of an organising character'. It is, as the title of Rose's book suggests, 'work' – part of the political process that at its hardest and least forgiving requires that you *'keep your mind in hell'*.

I have felt no greater possibility – whether cosmically, politically or trivially defined – than through love of the particular comrade with whom I share my life. In this sense the fear of replacement that marked my early adult years gives way to something more vital that is sometimes hell but more often not. To glimpse a possible other side to one's own replace-ability makes an engagement with its ugliness feel not only tolerable but perhaps even useful in some way.

The energy that animates a return to such thinkers as Kollontai and Gornick, unlike Freud's narcissistic drive to replace a lost *object*, is perhaps what Mark Fisher, following Derrida, described as a generative attachment to a cancelled vision of the future. As Fisher explained, the 'spectre of communism' described by Marx and Engels was a ghost of all tenses, 'a virtuality whose threatened coming was already playing a part in undermining the present state of things'.

As Gornick observes, the dogma that undid (actual) American Communism – as a distinct *no longer* rather than a possible *not yet* – was not the visionary Marxism that had allowed the impotent and isolated finally to 'see' themselves as part of something expansive. It was rather the ironic 'purging of the self' that came from excessive identification with the Party. As the Party came to stand in for an identity rather than a formation for organising around a shared political vision, it destroyed the Communist's ability, as Gornick puts it, 'to see himself in all those around him'.

To mourn the loss of Gornick's Communism would clearly amount to what Fisher, following

Freud, diagnosed as a fatal pattern – a traumatic and destructive 'compulsion to repeat'. It is perverse to wallow in longing for the loss of a failed political reality, a failed relationship, a lost plastic coffee scoop. It is important, however, to maintain a grip on lost futures – the ideals to which thwarted political formations rightly aspired, the kind of love that a now-lost boyfriend made you believe was possible.

If your first experience of employment was depressing too, and marked by the hazards of replacement, perhaps you have learnt that the opposite of depression is not happiness. If the Capgras patient, plagued by the horror of her own replacement, ends up believing that her real self is dead, then perhaps freedom from fear of replacement requires that we feel alive. This, it seems to me, is the opposite of depression, and is something I have felt most sharply when Forgetting the Idea of Being Special. When it is possible to feel replaceable not as a worker or a cluster of cells but as someone whose hopes and intentions for life are identical to those of others. No one should be made into a robot or inspired to make themselves a god. We are tired and sometimes hungry and have other things to do.

Bibliography

Books

Aristotle, *Physics*, 350 BCE
Nicholson Baker, *The Mezzanine*, 1988
Roland Barthes, *The Neutral*, 2002
— *Roland Barthes by Roland Barthes*, 1975
Aaron Benanav, *Automation and the Future of Work*, 2020
Lauren Berlant, *Cruel Optimism*, 2011
Eula Biss, *On Immunity*, 2014
Anne Boyer, *The Undying*, 2019
Nik Brown, *Immunitary Life*, 2018
Mikhail Bulgakov, *The Heart of a Dog*, 1925
Roberto Calasso, *The Ruin of Kasch*, 1983
Karel Čapek, *Rossums Universal Robots*, 1920
Jodi Dean, *Comrade*, 2019
Helen DeWitt, *Lightning Rods*, 2011

Homer, *Iliad*, c. 700 BCE

Mark Fisher, *Capitalist Realism*, 2009

Chris Kraus, *Aliens and Anorexia*, 2000

Franz Kafka, *The Trial*, 1925

Vivian Gornick, *The Romance of American Communism*, 1977

Ottessa Moshfegh, *My Year of Rest and Relaxation*, 2018

Maggie Nelson, *The Argonauts*, 2015

Sianne Ngai, *Theory of the Gimmick*, 2020

Lizzie O'Shea, *Future Histories*, 2019

Gillian Rose, *Love's Work*, 1995

Peter Sloterdijk, *Foams*, 2016

Plato, *Symposium*, 416 BCE

Isabel Waidner, *We Are Made of Diamond Stuff*, 2019

Simone Weil, *Gravity and Grace*, 1947

Articles/Essays

Walter Benjamin, 'The Work of Art in the Age
of Mechanical Reproduction', 1935
Roberto Esposito, 'The Biopolitics of Immunity
in Times of Covid', 2020
Sigmund Freud, 'On Narcissism', 1914
Mark Greif, 'Afternoon of the Sex Children', 2006
Alexandra Kollontai, 'Make Way for Winged
Eros: a letter to working youth', 1923
Chris Kraus, 'Resistance', 2008
Carolyn Lazard, 'How to Be a Person in the
Age of Autoimmunity', 2013
Henri Lefebvre, 'The Everyday and
Everydayness', 1987
Filippo Tommaso Marinetti and Luigi Colombo
Fillia, 'Manifesto of Futurist Cooking', 1930
New Masses Magazine, 'On the White
Collar Front', 1934
Paul B. Preciado, 'Forgetting the Idea of
Being Special', 2015
Amia Srinivasan, 'Stop the Robot Apocalypse',
2015

Poems

Adam Fitzgerald, 'The Lordly Hudson', 2015

Artworks

Helen Chadwick, *Blood Hyphen*, 1988
Revital Cohen & Tuur van Balen,
   The Immortal, 2012
Otobong Nkanga, *Recipe for Repairs*, 2019
Rosemarie Trockel, *Replace Me*, 2011

Films

Charlie Chaplain (dir.) *Modern Times*, 1936
Kitty Green (dir.), *The Assistant*, 2019
Fritz Lang (dir.) *Metropolis*, 1927

Acknowledgements

This short book was written over quite a long time with generous, patient and unfailingly humorous editorial input from Sam Fisher, Jake Franklin and especially Will Rees; its writing was in many ways a conversation with Will.

I'd like to acknowledge and big up those who read drafts or bits of drafts for various reasons, among them Anna Richmond, Lucy Brown-ridge and Freddie Bowerman. Your thoughts have been more than accidental to the finished entity.

Since this is my first book I would also like to thank my family. Particularly, my grandmother Marjorie Husain, an inspiring writer, and my parents Jamil and Erica. I'd also like to thank Dr Peta Fowler, who both made me consider writing and made me mark my own work when it was bad. I hope she will forgive me for my use of the Classics in this essay.

Finally thank you to Matt Huxley, without whom I would never have published anything good, or possibly anything at all.